START AND RUN A PROFITABLE
FREELANCE WRITING BUSINESS

START AND RUN A PROFITABLE
FREELANCE WRITING BUSINESS
Your step-by-step business plan

Christine Adamec, M.B.A.

Self-Counsel Press
a division of
International Self-Counsel Press Ltd.
Canada   U.S.A.

Printed in Canada

First edition: November, 1994; Reprinted: August, 1995

Canadian Cataloguing in Publication Data
      Adamec, Christine A., 1949 -
      Start and run a profitable freelance writing business
      (Self-counsel business series)

      ISBN 0-88908-523-4

      1. Authorship — Marketing. 2. Freelance journalism. 3. New business enterprises.
      I. Title. II. Series.
      PN153.A32 1994   808' .02   C94-910825-1

Self-Counsel Press
a division of
International Self-Counsel Press Ltd.

1481 Charlotte Road   1704 N. State Street
North Vancouver, British Columbia   Bellingham, Washington 98225
Canada V7J 1H1

CONTENTS

vi

SAMPLES

INTRODUCTION

No matter what people have told you, you *can* be a successful writer. It's neither impossible nor futile. I'm here to tell you why and show you how to succeed.

First, ask "Do I want to be a writer *and* make money? Is there is a writer inside me that needs to come out?"

Are you someone with interesting ideas and an intense curiosity about a subject or many different subjects? Have you pushed this side of you back into the shadows of your life because you equated writing with poverty?

Let that person out. If you want to launch a writing career and make some money, the good news is that these are not mutually exclusive goals, despite what you may have heard. In fact, there are plenty of opportunities today for writers, particularly in the non-fiction field. I'm talking about chances to exercise your creative talents and bring home some bucks.

Of course, you'll need to do some careful planning and learn how to effectively use your skills and abilities. It doesn't just happen. The purpose of this book is to get you started with the basics as well as give you some insider information that you won't read anywhere else.

Forget everything you've heard or read about the heavy competition, the difficulty obtaining assignments, and the paltry fees that lowly writers routinely receive. With effective marketing and basic business practices — which I'll discuss — you can and will earn good fees for your work.

Why? Because there are many editors, publishers, organizations, and individuals who need good writers. And sometimes they *desperately* need good writers.

In fact, according to a cover article in the February 1, 1994, issue of the *Wall Street Journal*, the demand for freelance writers is noticeably up in some areas. One temporary employment service in Chicago, Illinois, has opened a second office in San Francisco because of the need for writers.

You won't have to starve in a garret, no matter how romantic this image may appear to some. And you won't have to become a stereotypical artsy-craftsy "hippie" person. (Although you can continue this lifestyle if you choose!)

It is strange to me that the word "profit" has become a dirty word in society today. Yet, if entrepreneurs, including writers, cannot make a profit, they cannot pay their bills and have money left over.

I bring this up because freelance writing can be one of the most capitalistic of all endeavors. There are usually no set fees on what writers can earn on most jobs. It depends on how badly the client wants the job done, how fast he or she needs it, and how much you want to do it. What you get paid is a reflection of each. (I talk about setting fees and other related money issues later.)

Writers come from both poor and affluent backgrounds. Their ages range from twenty-something to retirement. (Some are teenagers!) Writers have an urgently needed skill, for which people will pay real money.

The life of the successful freelance writer can be thrilling and fulfilling, but it is also hard work. Sometimes you can get so involved in a project that you lose track of time, forget to eat, and maybe even forget to go to the bathroom. You immerse yourself in this job.

More often, however, you need to jump-start yourself, particularly on those days when you'd rather clean the cat litter than write a first draft. But the good writer writes the draft. (And cleans the litter later!)

There are sacrifices too, and in this book, I cover the basic advantages and disadvantages of a writing business and the nuts-and-bolts issues of running a successful business. It is important to know that the writing field is not necessarily easy and, frankly, it is not always fun.

But it can also be a great life and a profitable business if you manage it properly. Let that writer inside come on out! With this book, you can awaken the "inner you" and start on the path to success.

1
LIFE AS A FREELANCE WRITER: IS IT FOR YOU?

a. THE REALITY OF LIFE AS A WRITER

First, let's explore the idea of writing as a wonderfully glamorous career field, because this is a very prevalent stereotype. Prevalent, and for the most part, wrong.

The writing field is both more and less glamorous than the average person realizes. It is more glamorous because you get to meet important and influential people and ask questions that their friends and colleagues wouldn't dare ask. It is less glamorous because writing involves planning and hard work. If you've got a deadline to meet the next morning, you may still be up at 2:00 a.m. while everyone else in your family is enjoying a deep sleep. The glamour isn't there, only the work.

The typical scenario that many people imagine for their career as a freelance writer begins with their leisurely rise from bed at noon, yawning from the chic party attended the night before. After sorting through the many checks that have arrived in the mail, the writer considers whether to turn on the computer or take a "mental health" day off. After all, he or she is an important writer.

Yes, everyone knows that writers rush off and have many adventures and, once in a while, dash off something brilliant to satisfy their editors.

If your image of the writer corresponds to the above, you are in for a rude awakening. Accept up front that a freelance writing career isn't just a career; it's a business, and you won't succeed unless you're prepared to treat it like one.

If you're a flexible and curious person, as well as one who takes your work seriously, then a career as an entrepreneurial writer may be just right for you. Read on!

It is true that freelance writers are their own bosses and can turn down projects, enter new fields, and meet some very fascinating people in person or by phone. Being a freelance writer is (almost) never boring.

But there's a downside to freelance writing, and before plunging into this field, you need to look at both the positive aspects as well as the possible tradeoffs you may make in terms of income, time, and security.

b. ADVANTAGES

There are many advantages to being a freelance writer. You may already have considered some of these, but there are a few that may surprise you.

1. You're the boss

This is the number one plus for many freelance writers. You are in charge and you decide what to write about. By contrast, as a staff writer you might work in an office with a boss who treats you miserably. You have to grit your teeth, bear it, and soldier on.

But as a freelance writer, you can choose never to deal with an unreasonable person again. He or she is history. If you find a wonderful editor, you can develop a working relationship with that person that could last for months or even years. You decide who to work with, who is good, and who is bad. You're in charge.

2. You set your own schedule

As long as you meet your deadlines, you set your own schedule. If you want to finish a chapter at the crack of dawn, then you can. You are not constrained to work between 9:00 a.m. and 5:00 p.m. or any other set times. You make your own schedule and do not have to adapt to the norm. This is wonderful news for those of us who are naturally nocturnal.

3. It's fun

In the morning you may be interviewing a specialist in rare diseases and in the afternoon talking to a trade show director.

Your title of "freelance writer" or "journalist" or "entrepreneurial writer" or "contract writer" — or whatever you may prefer — gains you entry into many places the public never sees and opens up offers the average person will never receive.

Often, you gain behind-the-scenes access to people and businesses the general public cannot have. You get to describe what you see for them.

You can also travel extensively if you wish. For example, you could be a travel writer and make money by writing about the cruise you just took or the white water rafting adventure you plan to experience.

Or you can be an armchair writer and interview people all over the world by telephone, as I often do, asking them questions you need for a book, article, or report. (See chapter 9 for more about interviewing.)

4. You get paid for your work

When the mail arrives, there are checks with your name on them. It's a great feeling.

Although many people say they write for the sheer love of it, and would write for free, this book is for those who want to make money. Earning money is not inherently bad and those who write for low-paying markets are not necessarily morally superior.

On the other hand, it is not true that only best-selling authors pulling in the really big bucks are worth anything. Although I hope that my readers do become both famous and wealthy — if that's what they want — plenty of happiness and success can be found in a successful writing career.

How much money can you make? That is really up to you, the type of writing you do, your contacts, how prolific you are, and the contracts you create and sign. Usually you should not work for free *unless* you can identify a strong advantage in doing so.

For example, if you've just written a detailed book on anorexia nervosa, then you may wish to promote your book by writing free or low-paying articles for prestigious journals or publications that could lead to increased sales of your book.

When my first book (a how-to book on adoption) was published, I wrote articles for free for a nationwide adoptive parents' magazine, promoting my book and gaining strong name recognition for my writing.

But in most cases, it is more important that you are well paid for your hard work. (See chapter 10 for more about estimating what you should be paid.)

5. You save on expenses

You no longer need to rush around frantically in the morning to get ready for work and then drive through highly stressful bumper-to-bumper traffic to the big city. Think of all the time and stress you can avoid. Your blood pressure might even go down.

Bad weather? Not a problem. Generally, face-to-face interviews can be either rescheduled or conducted by telephone, fax, or on e-mail instead.

You also save on the wear and tear of your car, and all the gas, oil, and expenses related to daily commutes. Of course, freelance writers do need to travel sometimes, but you can request that travel expenses be added to your fee.

If you are writing a book, you can factor in projected expenses and decide whether to accept any money offered in advance. (For more about what to ask for in a writing contract, see chapter 10.)

You probably save on your clothing budget too. Many writers can wear whatever they want. If you're interviewing someone on the phone or typing up a manuscript, it doesn't matter if you have on a flannel nightgown or a T-shirt and shorts. Dress up or dress down; it's your choice.

Some people believe that people who work at home cannot be productive if they have on their "play clothes" and recommend that you dress for business. So if you can't produce without the "right" clothes on, go ahead and wear them.

Of course, when you go out to interview someone in person, you must dress professionally in appropriate business attire. Your aim is to be taken seriously.

6. You can pay more attention to your family

If family members are ill, you can stay home or take them to the doctor. No frantic negotiations with your boss, no worries about whether you have enough vacation set aside or if taking the day off will hurt your prospects for promotion. Rearranging your schedule is usually not a problem. If you have an interview set up that you cannot change, you'll have to work around it. The opportunity to attend to your family's needs when necessary is an advantage, especially for women. Now you don't have to put up with snide remarks about being on the "Mommy (or Daddy) track."

7. You get recognition

Virtually every writer is thrilled when the very first article or book is published with his or her name on it. You want to save it forever, frame it, show it to the whole world. Although it's not quite so dramatic the 200th or 500th time, it's still very nice to see your name in print.

Readers can also be very appreciative. Sometimes writers receive fan letters thanking them for their help in resolving a particular problem. Readers read your article or your book and something clicks. They try what you advise and it works. It is tremendously gratifying to receive such letters.

Books are reviewed; a favorable review can be a very heady experience. Good reviews will sell more copies of your book. You can also use them as a stepping stone to your next book contract.

Writers are often invited to talk about their book on the radio or appear on television. These are more opportunities to let people know about your ideas and expertise.

8. You can create your own work environment

You're usually not allowed to choose your coworkers in an office environment; someone else calls the shots. Coworkers — or your boss — can sometimes be annoying and intrusive, and the computer equipment at work may not be as good as the set-up you have at home.

At home, you decide how your office should be. You can have a room set aside for your work or you can use part of a room. Do you like plants hanging everywhere and scads of photos of your kids? Great! Do you do your best work while listening to rock or country music? No problem.

Choose the computer and office equipment that best suits your own needs. Buy an ergonomically correct chair that won't hurt your back, unlike that old, cheap, rigid one you were given back at the office.

9. It's a wonderful outlet for your own creativity

Writers seek out information and analyze and interpret it in an intriguing way that captures readers' attention. Writers have to come up with new ideas and angles for stories and present them in unique, memorable ways.

10. Writers can change lives

Maybe your profile of an elderly woman who returned to college to get her degree will subsequently inspire a middle-aged reader to feel that it is not too late to go back to school.

Words are very powerful. The children's nursery rhyme "Sticks and stones can break my bones, but names can never hurt me" has always puzzled me. Words can destroy and words can empower.

c. DISADVANTAGES

Nearly every profession has a downside. Often the negative aspects are a flip side of the positive ones.

1. You have to take full responsibility for your work

You *are* in charge and it's a good feeling to be "the boss," but you have to also take full responsibility. There's nowhere to hide in the hierarchy because it's just you. *You* must seek out work; *you* must fulfill your obligations.

Often it may seem that you have either not enough work or far too much. Many freelance writers have a considerable amount of trouble pacing themselves, a subject I discuss further in chapter 4.

If you don't have enough work, there's no boss to blame. If you have too much work to do, whose fault is that?

2. Planning your time is very important

Freelance writers must consider not only what is due today or this week, but also projects due next month or even three to six months from now.

In order to meet a deadline, a writer may need to talk to President Big from the XYZ Corporation within the next few weeks. And President Big's time must also be taken into account. Meeting your deadline may depend on whether President Big can fit you into his or her very busy work schedule.

If you're the kind of person who wrote all your term papers the night before they were due, you must break this habit immediately. Sometimes research can take weeks or months to do; it isn't always easy. When problems crop up, they must be resolved within a reasonable time frame.

3. Sometimes it's not fun

It's not always fun being a freelance writer, but if it's a career that suits you, it is fun most of the time. For example, let's say you have a cold and don't feel like interviewing the important person who has deigned to speak with you.

But this is the only time to do it; it's now or never. So you do it. First, you give yourself a strong pep talk about how much you really want to do it. Then you put on your best "smiley-face" voice and do the interview.

Some aspects of writing are not fun. The most hated duties vary among writers. For me, writing first drafts has always been an exercise in torture. It's just no fun at all! But once I have something typed into my computer, even if it's gobbledygook, most of the time I can fix it.

Other writers don't like to edit their own work. They also find it painful to take out wonderful quotations that unsympathetic editors may feel really don't add anything to the story or that make it too long. A good writer grits his or her teeth and takes out that extraneous material before submission, no matter how flowing, alliterative, or just plain great it seems. If it doesn't fit, out it goes.

4. Earnings are generally sporadic

Freelance writers rarely, if ever, receive a weekly or biweekly paycheck. Instead, the checks come when they are due according to the contracts you've worked out. (And sometimes they DON'T come when they are due, an issue addressed in chapter 10.)

I have received a check for $6,000 on one day and then nothing for eight weeks. When this kind of thing happens, you need to plan so that your cash flow is as steady as you can make it. You need some amount of money to cover your overhead over the lean periods and make a profit as well.

You need to plan. Don't rush out and spend a big fat check if you're going to need money later on! (This is hard not to do, but it is very necessary.)

5. No company benefits

Unlike full-time employees working for others who receive a paid vacation, paid sick time, and so forth, self-employed business people don't receive such benefits. If you don't work, you don't get paid. So if you want to take a vacation for several weeks, you may need to carefully budget your time and money.

6. You must negotiate contracts and fees

Keep in mind that this is a business and you should use or develop business skills. Many people dislike talking about money and negotiating contracts, but freelance writers have to do this.

It may not be genteel or fun, but your earnings are what you make them. And remember, writers provide a service, just like printers, publishers, lawyers, and other professionals. Never forget this.

7. Record keeping

Writers need to track their expenses as well as their revenues. Record keeping is tedious but it is essential. How else can you know how much to bill editors for your phone expenses if you don't know who you called or when you called?

Some writers just don't see the importance of tracking their business expenses, but if you don't know where your money is going, how can you make adjustments? How can you learn from your mistakes?

For example, you may look at your expenses for paper over the course of three months and find out you've been buying paper on an as-needed basis — whenever you run out. This may have been about once a month. Realizing this, you might decide it could make sense to buy your paper in larger quantities so you can get a better price. Cutting expenses is another way to improve your "bottom line." (See chapter 11 for more on record keeping.)

8. Self-promotion

Marketing both you and your ideas can be difficult sometimes. Too many people are incredibly modest about their talents and are far too reluctant to broadcast their skills. Although you do not need to convince every editor that you are the greatest human who ever lived, you should convey the idea that you are a talented and creative person who can do the job and can do it well. Extreme modesty is no virtue in a freelance writer.

9. Rejection

Can you tolerate rejection? I contend that writers must cultivate the armor of an armadillo because rejections come with the territory. When someone rejects your work, you must keep in mind that it is usually not personal and it is not you who is being rejected.

Your work may have been turned down because it just didn't fit. It wasn't what was wanted or needed. Maybe you chose the wrong market. Or maybe the editor was dead wrong. However, like it or not, he or she is empowered with the decision-making authority. Calling the editor to try to talk him or her out of rejecting your idea or manuscript is usually self-defeating or degrading. Don't do it.

There are many reasons for rejections. The only common denominator is that all writers, no matter how experienced, must face them. A successful freelance writer does not need constant pats on the back and can take the rejections that come. They hurt briefly, they are disappointing, and they're also inevitable.

Sometimes what you've proposed doesn't suit the editor and you cannot fix it. So you regroup. Take a hard look at it, decide if it might suit another publication, and send it off. Some writers have had their book proposals rejected 50 times, but they kept submitting it because they were convinced the book was important and needed. By submission number 51, it may sell. Or it may not. Some projects need to be set aside for awhile.

Getting angry when you don't receive a rapid reply from an editor or client is another waste of your valuable time. "Some writers get out of kilt if their queries don't get answered quickly," says Dana Cassell, publisher of *Freelance Writer's Report* and an experienced writer.

"The writers I have seen over the years who have been successful don't get upset if they don't get responses. Instead, they have a routine and they follow up after so many weeks. Successful writers look at rejections as a fact and they realize that it's a numbers game." A percentage of your queries and the work itself will be accepted, and as you gain experience, that percentage will increase.

Cassell says writers need to understand that in the business world, not everyone buys. "Freelance writing is no different. But too many times, people look at the creative end of it and forget that writing is also a business."

10. Setting boundaries

Although you can usually pay more attention to your family and friends, sometimes a writer needs to concentrate completely on his or her work. This may be hard for people to understand at first. After all, you're home, so you're not doing anything, right?

Relatives may want to visit and chat. They may find it difficult to understand that you have a deadline to meet and must finish your article or chapter now to meet your schedule. (This is a very common problem shared by everyone who works from his or her home.)

Polite but firm explanations are in order. Explain to drop-in visitors that even though you are at home, you are also at work. And it is not a cute little hobby or something to fill your time; it is your career and your vocation.

Many writers are shocked to find they must still budget time for child care, especially for children who are infants and toddlers or preschoolers. You don't want the CEO of a large corporation to hear your child in the background saying, "I go potty now?" Charming to you, maybe, but not to everyone else.

On the other hand, sometimes a client may call you at 9:00 p.m. or later when your children are clamoring for attention. In that case, a client should be appropriately apologetic and understanding. You do, after all, have a life!

Balancing the demands of work and family can be particularly demanding for a writer, especially one with school-age or younger children. Often clients do call after 5:00 p.m., especially if they are in a different time zone. They'll also call during lunch, dinner, and just about anytime.

What's the way around this? Your answering machine. The answering machine can screen your calls. If it's important and you are at home, then you can pick up.

11. Recognition isn't guaranteed

Often the level of recognition you seek is not immediately forthcoming or may not occur for years. Or ever! We can't all be best-selling authors. So if you are looking for fame and notoriety, and these are your primary motivations for starting your writing business, think again. Making a profit is certainly within reach but fame is far more fleeting and unpredictable.

Many successful writers turn out pieces for trade publications on a regular basis; there are hundreds of magazines oriented to a particular field or area of interest. An article for a trade magazine will not be read by all your friends and colleagues — unless they are in a particular field.

Many people think they could write "if only I had the time." They feel that anybody could do it. One professional writer who was told by his doctor that he'd like to be a writer if he had only had some "extra time" retorted to the doctor that, yes, he'd like to be a physician — if he only had some spare time. The doctor got the message: time is only one factor.

Give yourself the positive feedback you need because you can't always depend on kind words from editors, readers, friends or relatives, and colleagues.

Sometimes editors and readers disagree with what a writer says. Some may not like it, for various reasons. You learn to live with it and you learn from it.

12. It can get lonely

Probably every writer finds the solitary nature of writing for a living difficult at times. True, you may be interviewing people on the phone all day long and not have a moment to spare. But there is no office banter, no kidding around at the coffee machine, and none of the latest gossip.

One solution is to get out and meet with friends for lunch, join clubs, and remain an active person. Some writers become so obsessed about production that they run the risk of becoming recluses. This is a big mistake.

13. Delusions of instant wealth

Do you aspire to great wealth? If this is your primary motivation in life, please don't become a writer! Although you should be able to make a profitable living, it is also important to keep in mind that the six- or seven-figure book advances are *very* few and far between. That is why they make the big headlines in *Publisher's Weekly*.

Most small business people don't expect to break even (when your earnings equal your expenses) for about a year or so and sometimes longer, because they anticipate that they have to learn the business, create new contacts, and build up their client base. So you should plan to have sufficient funds to fall back on when you start your career as a writer.

d. WHO HIRES WRITERS AND WHY

There are many reasons why writers are needed and why you can succeed in the field of publishing, with persistence and hard work.

Sadly, it appears that fewer and fewer people learn how to write effectively in school or college. This shortfall of talent and experience has increased the demand for effective communicators because editors and business people who hire writers must select from a diminishing pool of talent.

Here are just a few of the types of markets that may suit your particular skills and services.

1. Corporations and businesses

With the downsizing and layoffs in many major corporations, there are increasing opportunities for work to be contracted out to writers. By using a freelancer, the company can get a fast turnaround, pay a flat rate, and avoid extra costs for benefits (i.e., vacation time, sick time, and so forth).

Corporations publish monthly newsletters, reports, news releases, and all sorts of communications. They may depend on writers to produce one article or sometimes all the copy for an entire newsletter. They want good writers who can produce material rapidly.

Many businesses and organizations need writers who can produce articles for in-house publications. They often don't advertise this need because they operate on a referral basis and call upon writers infrequently. These opportunities can become very lucrative for writers.

And don't forget small business people. They need news releases, copy for pamphlets, and a variety of written communications. You might find your niche writing for the local business people in your area.

Associations and small business people need writers to assist them with public relations — writing news releases, articles about their business to submit to trade publications, and business brochures and pamphlets.

Businesses also use ghost writers to prepare special reports, proposals, and articles. (A ghost writer does not receive a byline; that is, your name doesn't appear on the piece.) Businesses want you to do the research and writing but don't want your name to appear because you're not a "big name" in the field and you are not on staff. The name of someone within the company is given as the "author" of the piece. Or no author is credited at all. But your name appears on the check!

With the increasing popularity of desktop publishing, many large and small companies have launched newsletters. Often they don't have the time to write or edit the articles, so they contract the work out. This is another very good opportunity for the writer who can "write tight" and turn around copy quickly.

In a related field, many businesses need video scriptwriters. Videos may be used for training, promotion, or a wide variety of purposes. The skills needed for script writing are different from those needed for magazine feature writing, because writers must take into account the visual aspect and other elements, but they are learnable and this field can be very lucrative.

2. Technical industries

If you've ever tried to decipher what in the world your computer manual means, you can easily understand why the world needs more technical writers. You don't have to be an engineer or a "techie" to write manuals or a wide array of technical communications for companies or publishers. What you *do* need is the ability to learn what the readers need to know and to express the information as simply and clearly as possible.

Technical writers explain how to perform a procedure or how to comply with new government regulations, for example, in plain language. Or they may provide many other types of communications that demand writers.

Some tech writers find jobs on their own while others seek out jobs with temporary service agencies or agencies that specialize in technical writing assignments. (See the Appendix for a partial listing of such agencies.)

3. Trade magazines

Trade magazines are always looking for good writers. Trade magazines are specific to a field; there are trade magazines for artists, physicians, paralegals, and many other trades. Take a look at the current edition of the *Writer's Market* to see how many trade magazines they describe — and understand that this reference book only skims the surface!

You don't need to be an artist or a physician if you have the ability to interview people and get interesting and vital information, This is a skill that can be learned.

(Sometimes you may need to convince the trade editor you can learn quickly and get a handle on what is needed to write about a particular field. For more about talking to editors, see chapter 7.)

4. Health care organizations and consultants

Health care organizations and health care consultants need writers, especially now. A changing health care field means there is a strong demand for medical/business writers. You don't have to be a doctor or nurse to interview doctors, nurses, and medical researchers about their work. Most medical experts are very pleased to share their knowledge — although pinning them down to a specific time isn't always easy.

In the United States, changing rules regarding insurance coverage and possible radical changes in the health care field will continue to create a strong need for good writers for at least the next five years.

New technology in the health and medical sector also offers more opportunities for writers. Every new development or critical issue in the health field in North America needs a writer to explain it. In some cases, the rest of the world is your readership. (Yes, there are global markets as well.)

Another important point to keep in mind is that with the aging of the population, and the huge bulge of baby boomers entering middle age and beyond, more and more people will seek and need information on medical treatments, insurance coverage, and other issues. Benefits firms, consultants, newsletter publishers, and other markets need medical and business writers.

5. Consumer magazines

Consumer magazines — those popular magazines you see on the rack at your local market — need writers too. The more well-known publications are also more difficult markets to penetrate, particularly for the novice writer, but if you have a unique idea or local slant that might interest many others, then you should give it a try.

Popular consumer magazines generally pay well and pay "on acceptance," as opposed to "on publication." But if you expect to hang your whole career on writing solely for magazines with very high name recognition, think again. Few writers concentrate all their efforts on writing for the glossy magazines you see at your local newsstand.

6. Individuals

Many individuals independently seek the services of ghost writers because they may have a unique story they cannot write effectively themselves. Or they may need a manuscript polished. I was hired by a woman who wanted to win the "Mother of the Year" prize offered by an organization. I wrote her resume. She won the prize. Others may hire you to assist them with a book proposal or to write the book itself, or both.

7. Self-publishing

Self-publishing is another option, whether you wish to create your own newsletter, reports, or even publish a book yourself. Some self-publishers have later sold their books to established publishers — while others have faded into obscurity. I discuss this option more in chapter 5.

8. Project fixing

Another opportunity for many writers lies in taking over projects that others have dropped for a variety of reasons. Often editors, business people, and those who hire ghost writers in such situations need good writers to "fix" or rewrite manuscripts — sort of "manuscript doctors." I have taken over chapters that needed to be rewritten, reports that were started and dropped, and many other projects started by others.

The good news about taking over someone else's project is that the customer is often so dissatisfied with it and so frustrated that practically anything you do will be perceived as wonderful.

The bad news is that by the time the customer finds you, he or she is often frantic to get the job done immediately and, therefore, cannot give you much time at all.

With all these opportunities, why not rush out and tell your corporate boss what you really think of him or her, and then quit and launch your career as a writer? Resist the temptation. It's not always a good idea to quit your day job right away. It is better to test the water first rather than plunge right in. (For more about making the transition from full-time employment to freelance writer, see chapter 3.) First, you need to carefully assess your suitability for the life of a full-time writer.

e. ESSENTIAL TRAITS FOR THE SUCCESSFUL WRITER

1. Talent

Talent is important; you may have it, but not know it. If you've never been published before, this doesn't mean you don't have talent. What it means is you've never been published before. So how do you know if you have the ability to be a writer?

(a) Look at your past

Did you receive good grades on term papers in high school or college? (This is NOT a prerequisite for success!) Did you enjoy writing? What were the achievements you were most proud of? Did they have anything to do with any or all of the elements of professional writing: library research, interviewing, analyzing material, as well as writing it up?

(b) Look at the present

Do you write letters to the editors of newspapers or magazines? Do you wonder about issues that don't get mentioned in articles and sometimes become annoyed because reporters leave out facts you think are important?

(c) Do you love to read?

Most good writers are voracious readers who pick up words, phrases, and ideas from a variety of material, often unconsciously.

(d) Look at yourself

Do you think you exhibit some or all of the following qualities? If you do, you have the potential to be a good writer.

2. Tenacity

Tenacity is another necessary quality for a successful writer.

Profit-making writers are persistent and don't give up easily. If a writer can't find needed information from one source after at least a few tries, he or she tries other sources. If a very good story idea is turned down by an editor, the persistent writer gives other editors the chance to learn about this great idea. If at first you don't succeed, persist, persist, and persist.

Sometimes interviewees are reluctant to share important information. The successful writer works hard to convince them that the information is needed and will be handled properly and fairly.

3. Self-direction

Maybe you can lead others, but can you be self-directed? Are you a task-oriented person?

Although many editors offer guidelines, helpful hints, and sometimes even leads (e.g., contacts or prospective interviewees), the successful writer makes his or her own plan and researches other contacts and information when needed.

4. Ability to put yourself in someone else's shoes

A good writer can put himself or herself in the shoes of the readers, whether they are doctors, lawyers, or cashiers in a supermarket. What are the readers' primary concerns? What do they care about?

5. Ability to be self-critical, but not self-blaming

As the writer researches and drafts an article, he or she must constantly ask, does this ring true? Is this clear? Am I leaving anything important out? This is not an internal harangue but rather a zeroing-in on areas that you could improve.

6. Organizational ability

Can you read three or more different articles and find a common thread? Can you keep track of what you are doing and for whom? (This will probably not be a problem right away, but as you become more successful, you need to pace yourself.)

Writers don't have to be perfectionists but they should be able to have some kind of filing system — even if they are the only ones who can understand it!

7. A willingness to network

The more adept you are at obtaining contacts through contacts you've already made, and at leapfrogging (in an organized way) from one expert to another, the better you will be at both obtaining assignments and at researching those assignments.

For example, each time you interview a person, you should ask if there is anyone else in the field that he or she can recommend that you talk to. Be sure to ask for that person's phone number. Most people are amazingly helpful about opening up their Rolodexes to interviewers and researchers. You save an incredible amount of time and energy when you are able to get contacts this way. Often personal referrals can lead you to people you'd never have found on your own.

When you find those people, tell them who recommended that you call and also ask for more contacts. If you don't know how to network with people, learn. (See chapter 8 for more about networking.)

8. Ability to meet deadlines

Missing deadlines is a key reason why new writers ultimately fail. They lose clients because of lateness and find it difficult to develop new ones.

If an editor or other customer is counting on your book, article, or newsletter and it is not completed in time, you won't last long with that editor. Don't give stories tantamount to "the dog ate my homework."

Sometimes you'll have a valid reason for not meeting a deadline, and in this case, you may be able to work out a solution with your client. For example, I have given an editor all my research notes when I was unable to complete an assignment due to a sudden illness in my family.

It is true that sometimes editors give you a deadline that isn't the "real" deadline. They've generally been burned in the past by procrastinating writers who turned in their work late or failed to turn it in at all.

After working with you awhile and learning to trust you, editors eventually tell you what the real "drop-dead" date is.

9. Good listening skills

Do people like to talk to you? Are you sometimes surprised at how much people reveal to you? Congratulations, you are probably a very good listener. If not, don't worry. It's a learnable skill and writers have plenty of opportunities to practice.

Although most people presume they are extremely effective at listening since they possess two ears and normal hearing, most people are poor listeners. Scientists have proven that much of what is said to us doesn't penetrate at all because we are attending to our inner thoughts or outer distractions. We also think faster than another person can speak.

We unconsciously know this, and what happens is we start to tune out the speaker, presuming we'll come back "on time." But sometimes we become so caught up in our own thoughts, that when we do tune in to the speaker again, he or she has gone far beyond the point where we last listened.

As a result, the ineffective listener can miss valuable information. Good writers cannot afford to make this mistake too often. (See chapter 9 for more about becoming an effective listener.)

When you interview someone, your listening skills are tremendously valuable because you can pick up the non-verbal cues that say what the person really feels but has not said. If you are a good listener, you detect each nuance of the person's voice. You are aware when they hesitate. The person's body language and posture reveal his or her feelings as well. The good listener pays attention to these signals and gains insight and information.

10. Empathy

Are you the kind of person people like to talk to? As an interviewer, you need to elicit information from a very wide assortment of people. Can people open up to you? You don't need to be a psychologist or social worker. But a basic liking of people is essential to a successful writing career, in my opinion.

11. Assertiveness

A successful writer must have or develop the ability to step forward and say "I can do this job." Many of us have been trained not to blow our own horn.

It may seem both immodest and tacky, but how is anyone going to know you're available and you're good unless you say so? As a result, if you don't feel that you have the self-confidence to assert yourself, you need to cultivate it.

12. Good family relationships

Another aspect that is important to the success or failure of your venture is your family, particularly if you are married or have a "significant other" in your life.

Will that person be supportive of your goals? Will he or she understand that just because you are home doesn't mean you can always pick up the clothes at the cleaners, do the grocery shopping, and so on?

Will he or she understand that sometimes deadlines mean you will have to work nights, weekends, and sometimes on holidays too? Conversely, you mustn't take advantage of his or her ability to be understanding and supportive and allow your work to spill over into the time you spend together.

Taking on a writing business will bring changes to your life. Changes send out ripples that affect your family. So there may be an adjustment period until your family understands the new role you have chosen.

Be sure to establish an office area that is NOT readily available to your spouse, friends, or children. I recommend this as a safety measure.

A friend who formerly ran a mail order business let her son play computer games on the same computer where she had stored her entire mailing list of 5,000 names, which, alas, she had failed to back up.

A virus on her child's game destroyed all her data and was the beginning of the end of her business. It was not the child's fault; I'm sure he felt terrible. But the lesson to be learned here is to treat your own work seriously and that is one step toward having your family treat it seriously too.

In the next chapter, I talk about launching your new business, and what you need to do to get started, including the mental and physical tools needed. Before you read on, however, see Worksheet #1 below. This worksheet can help you evaluate whether you have the potential and whether you are suited to becoming a freelance writer.

WORKSHEET #1
SELF-EVALUATION

Answer each question to help you assess your potential for success in running a freelance writing business.

	Frequently	Sometimes	Rarely
1. You love to read.	_____	_____	_____
2. You're curious.	_____	_____	_____
3. You like to ask questions.	_____	_____	_____
4. You get your work done on time.	_____	_____	_____
5. You like to make your own schedule.	_____	_____	_____
6. You think fast and can improvise.	_____	_____	_____
7. You're a good listener: people open up to you.	_____	_____	_____
8. You can be alone for hours.	_____	_____	_____

If at least six or seven of your answers are "frequently," then I'd say you're on your way to success! If most of your answers are "sometimes," especially five or more, then you may need to consider whether you can reshape yourself. Some people can. If most of your answers are "rarely," you should seriously reconsider whether you truly wish to become a writer.

2
GETTING STARTED

Now that you have a basic idea of the breadth of potential markets, the lifestyle, and the skills and abilities needed to be a successful freelance writer — and you believe that you can be successful — what's next? First, you need to adopt the proper attitude.

a. THE WRITER'S MIND-SET

Many people new to the publishing field are very timorous and shy and this is understandable. Your first day on the job as a teacher, lawyer, or cashier in the local supermarket can be nerve-racking. The problem is that many writers take far too long to get themselves into the writer's mind-set. What is this mysterious mind-set? It is a combination of attitudes that motivate behavior and enable a writer to succeed. Here is what you should cultivate.

1. Self-acceptance

Accept yourself as a writer and also as a competent writer. Don't say "I'm a writer?" with a question mark on the end. Neither should you over-dramatize it with an exclamation mark.

Some people probably fear actually saying that they're writers because they haven't yet been published, or have *only* had five pieces published, or *only* one book, or *only* fiction or *only* non-fiction, and so on. You are a writer if you say you are a writer, in my opinion. Maybe not a published writer yet, but a writer nonetheless.

Your goal, as a writer, is to be published and paid and to make a profit. As you work toward that goal, you *are* a writer.

This may sound silly but what I've told some of my former writing students to do is to say to themselves over and over, "I'm a writer" until it no longer sounds unnatural. You should try this too. Then tell five people you know that you're a writer. Most of them will not be shocked, nor will they challenge you.

Some may scoff. So what? You may be surprised to learn that many people are quite envious and wish that they could say they are writers too. A lawyer friend informed me, to my astonishment, that it was far more prestigious to be a writer than it is to be a lawyer.

2. Humility

But aren't self-acceptance and humility mutually exclusive traits? I don't think so. When I refer to humility, I'm talking about the willingness to ask questions that you think might sound "stupid" and to venture into areas where you will sometimes have to strain your brain. Because if you don't ask those questions, you run the very real risk of shortchanging your readers later on.

3. Businesslike attitude

Acknowledge that this is, after all, a business. Which means that in most cases, you will not go out, interview anyone you feel like, write an article or book, and then seek out someone to publish your piece. This is the mark of a true amateur.

Instead, the writer finds unique and marketable ideas and offers them to an editor or client in the form of a "query" or "proposal." After receiving a go-ahead from a customer, the professional writer researches and writes the piece.

4. A willingness to look at the world from other perspectives

Many new writers erroneously assume that if they are interested in a subject, the whole world will share this enthusiasm. But this is just not true. We live in a very diverse society and the editors and publishers who succeed are well aware of who their readers are — how old they are, how affluent, what interests them, and much more.

Even if you have an idea that seems just right for a specific publication, an editor may know of key people that he or she would like interviewed. If you've already researched and written the article, you've done a lot of extra work for no extra pay.

So maximize your business by finding ideas you'd like to write about and ideas you have good reasons to believe people would like to read about. You'll need to get into the habit of asking who this subject would appeal to. Would this subject be intriguing to adolescents or the aged? To people fascinated by politics or intrigued by beautiful art?

Often you will find the same research can be used over and over by rethinking how it could interest a different audience of readers.

5. An understanding of what the product is

Understand that it is not you who is the product! Let me explain. A major misconception I hear frequently is this: that your pay for writing should be equivalent to how many advanced degrees you have earned and how much work experience you have gained. Well, it usually doesn't work that way in this field.

You need to understand how being an entrepreneurial writer is very different from being an employee. This is a big attitudinal leap, and let me illustrate with an example. I was contacted by a man who asked me what a 50-year-old engineer with 30 years' experience is "worth" as a technical writer; that is, how much should he charge for his work?

He was asking the wrong question! Your experience level is only part of the equation — it is primarily the job itself that must be evaluated, and every job is different depending on how long it is, how much research is required, how fast it must be done, and other factors. These factors vary greatly, depending on who does the job and who assigns the job, and sometimes writers get frustrated because there are no set answers in many cases.

When you apply for a full-time job as an employee, you are the product. There is usually a fairly narrow salary range the employer will pay.

When you seek a freelance assignment, it is the job itself that is paramount. The client has to consider whether this assignment is needed. Does it fit into his or her overall game plan? What kind of budget is available? These are the questions you should ask prospective clients.

I have seen people with Ph.D.s in English fall flat on their face in the field of freelance writing, not because they weren't gifted at writing, but because they were unskilled at the art of simple business practices and were unwilling to learn. They refused to work with customers who would not agree with their conception of a project.

This is also why people with high school diplomas or college degrees in all sorts of disciplines can succeed at writing. It is writing talent combined with the willingness to work with a customer that is so badly needed.

Another aspect of being an entrepreneurial writer versus being an employee is the timeliness of projects. Generally, clients want to hire you for what you can do for them now, as in right now or within the next 30 days or so. If you apply for a job as an employee, your skills and talents are considered as well as what the employer thinks you will be able to do for the firm over the long term.

But when you are hired on as an entrepreneurial writer, you are needed to solve a particular problem or to do a particular job, not to perform over the next year or next few years.

The client knows that he or she can hire you for this job and never use you again if you don't work out. Thus, it is how you are perceived as a solution to a problem, rather than you as an ongoing asset to the business, which is important.

b. POSITION YOURSELF AS A SOLUTION

How can you position yourself as a solution? That depends on many factors. If you have a new idea for a magazine, for example, your solution is to provide the editor with interesting copy that also fits in well with the magazine's other material.

If you are hired to rewrite badly written text for a publisher, you are the solution because you can improve material that they need.

So you must also get at least part way into the mind-set of your client. Try to brainstorm about the client's problems and how you can help solve them. One way to do this is to review material published in the past and see how you could do it differently or better.

So instead of asking a blanket question about how much you are worth, understand that your "worth" is highly dependent on the client and how much he or she is willing to pay you. It is a very market-driven system.

c. PRESENT A PROFESSIONAL ATTITUDE

Never forget that when an editor hires you for a magazine or business assignment, you are representing his or her company. Even though you are a freelancer, the people you interview will automatically associate your attitude, appearance, and overall behavior with the publication. Be professional in every way.

Some editors have complained that they have been embarrassed by freelance writers they hired who showed up to interview people dressed sloppily and with a very careless attitude. Think of your clients as your customers. The people you interview are likely to be their customers.

d. WRITERS HAVE SEVERAL CUSTOMERS

Writers have several very different customers — first the editor and/or the publisher, and second, the readers.

Although the mating habits of armadillos may be compelling reading to you, consider whether it would appeal to your editor and subsequently your readers. What do they want to know? What would they be curious about?

To truly understand your customers, do your homework by reading other materials put out by the publisher or solicited by the editor. Analyze who the readers are as well.

e. GETTING DOWN TO BASICS: STARTING YOUR BUSINESS

1. Choosing a name

Most writers choose to operate under their own name. You can also choose to have a business name (e.g., Creative Enterprises). Your local business authority can tell you about what is required to register your business name. Your bank can help you set up a checking account under that name as well.

Although you could choose to incorporate, most writers operate as sole proprietorships, which means the business is entirely in the writer's name rather than the name of a corporate entity.

Unless you plan to create or extend your business into a public relations firm, I see no advantage in establishing your business under any name other than your own. Most prospective customers will quickly realize that you are a one-person operation. Calling yourself something like International Communications is unlikely to generate more assignments for you.

2. Tools of the writing trade

There are certain basic tools of the trade that every successful writer needs. These are tools that enable you to effectively research and produce your work and also communicate with others.

(a) A computer

The days of pounding out copy on an old typewriter are over for the writer who expects to earn a decent living. Face it: your competition uses computers and word processing programs and you should too.

This is not a book about what kind of computer or word processing program to buy. Models and prices change too quickly and I'm not an expert in the field. I use an IBM-compatible computer with WordPerfect 6.0 software and a Hewlett Packard laser printer. However, I acknowledge that other computers and programs work very well.

A "mouse" isn't necessary for word processing, but some writers prefer them. A mouse lets you move around the screen very rapidly and cut and paste large chunks of text.

(b) A printer

You can generally ignore what publications like *The Writer's Market* say about using or not using a dot matrix printer. (This is the kind of printer that forms copy by creating tiny little dots.)

Today, text produced on a dot matrix printer is indistinguishable from text produced on a letter quality printer. If you think an editor is going to get out a magni-

fying glass to see if there are little dots or not, think again.

On the other hand, if your dot matrix printer is ten years old, you may wish to purchase a newer model. Prices for basic printers are fairly reasonable today.

I use a laser printer because I also produce a monthly newsletter. I need the laser printer to create graphics, different layouts, and varied font styles. Prices on laser printers have dropped in the past few years and may be within your price range.

(c) Software

You need some kind of word processing program to do your work, and there are many good products available. Determine what your needs are, check out a few possibilities at a local computer store, ask around, and then buy what suits you the best. I use WordPerfect 6.0 and it works for me. You may prefer another program.

(d) A modem

A modem links your computer to your telephone and enables you to communicate with other computers and such online computer services as CompuServe, GEnie, Prodigy, the Internet, and an amazing array of bulletin boards. In an increasing number of cases, editors and clients request you to transmit the material electronically to their own bulletin boards, particularly when your client is a newspaper editor.

It is not yet a necessity to go online, but more and more editors are asking writers to file stories electronically, sometimes through electronic services and sometimes directly to the client's own computer. (Reporters file stories off-line in this manner.) Still, many are satisfied if you can send them a disk through the mail that they can read.

(e) A database

I consider my on-line searching of databases to be a "tool" of my trade because it enables me to locate information very quickly at virtually any time. A database is

17

a compendium of information; for example, there are databases of legal journals, medical journals, and a broad array of publications.

A person searches these databases using special "key words" related to the subject area. For example, if I were searching for information on modems, I would probably use the word "modem" as a key word.

I also have obtained many assignments by reading general messages on CompuServe open to all readers, such as "Need Writer! $800 per Chapter!" (This was really a message I responded to. I negotiated telephone expenses as an add-on and wrote two chapters for a frantic businessperson who needed the work done in a hurry.)

(f) A fax machine

My sales went up after I bought my fax machine. Why? Because now when I call an editor with an idea, I can fax my clips right away if requested. (Don't fax long documents without permission. It can be very annoying to the recipient to have his or her fax machine tied up.)

I have presented an idea to an editor who was a total stranger to me, been told to fax some clips, and been assigned a story within two hours. Of course, it doesn't always work out this way. But it can.

Do you lack clips (published samples of your work) to send? When I started out, I used old term papers to demonstrate my writing ability to prospective customers. So why not fax a few pages of some writing you are proud of?

Do remember, however, that when you are sending only a part of a manuscript or article, you should let the recipient know, so he or she doesn't think the rest of it got lost somewhere. You can either mention this on a cover sheet or jot a note on the first page you send.

If you can't afford to buy a fax machine, you may be able to buy a fax card and associated software for your computer. Or, you could arrange with a local business-person, such as a small printer, to accept your faxes and to allow you to send faxes for a nominal fee. If you do this, be sure that he or she understands you must be immediately notified if something comes in for you!

A big advantage of a fax is it speeds up the whole process and you don't have to depend on "snail mail," a term some people use to refer to postal service.

My fax machine doubles as an answering machine and can recognize whether it hears a screechy tone of an incoming fax or the sound of a voice. If the person calling wants to send a fax after leaving a message, he or she can.

I also receive faxes from my editors, who send me everything from names of people they want interviewed to actual contracts. I have also received unsolicited offers to do stories via my fax line. Put your fax number on your letterhead, underneath your regular telephone number. It makes you appear very serious about your work. (And you are, aren't you?)

(g) An answering machine

You can use the one you have now but get rid of the kiddie messages and stupid jingles, etc. Keep your message brief and to the point. Answering machines can capture important assignments you would otherwise miss out on, messages from editors, and so on. You may be able to buy an answering machine that also doubles as a fax machine.

Use an answering machine as your voice mail. Make your message clear and simple.

Make sure all your friends and relatives know that the telephone will be answered with the message that you have chosen, so that they won't hurriedly hang up if they should call to leave a message. They can also notify key people in their lives that it's okay to leave a message on the machine.

You may also wish to leave the machine on while you are home and working. The phone can be a terrible distraction for a writer facing a deadline, and you may decide that you will only pick up if it's an emergency.

(h) A telephone

This is the most obvious tool, but you don't want to forget it! It's okay to use your home phone as your work phone, but get an extension so you can talk in your office area, away from the family and with a little more privacy. Some writers prefer to pay for a separate line, so editors won't hear busy lines because your teenager is talking to a friend.

Some telephone services offer an array of choices. For example, I use a telephone company service (AT&T) that takes a message for me if my phone is busy. As a result, I don't "busy out" important calls. It costs me about $5 a month and is well worth it.

Some writers have their calls "bounced" to other lines. Others use "call waiting," which gives you a signal when you are on a call to let you know that you have another call. I personally find this service intrusive and distracting, but others find it very valuable.

Some writers pay extra so they can code their telephone bills. For example, typing "11" for one client, "12" for another, and so on. They keep a record of which client belongs to which number. When they get the telephone bill, they can add up all the 11s and bill the client, and so on.

The problem is that this doesn't tell you who each call was to. Often editors or other clients request verification of your expenses, generally in the form of an itemized listing of who you called and when, along with a copy of your telephone bill.

It can be very tricky reconstructing a record of all your calls months after you have finished an assignment. As a result, I recommend recording all long-distance calls.

(i) A copier

Although most writers don't have a photocopying machine, prices are coming down drastically and if you can afford one, you may find it to be a good investment. A copier allows you to photocopy your clips, magazine articles, and many other documents and avoid a trip to the local copy center.

There are also fax machines that can photocopy documents.

(j) A desk

Get a desk that is not too low or too high. Your hands should be able to be loose at your sides and not straining upwards or down. For some reason, many people put their computers too high up and risk neck strain. Lower is better.

(k) A file cabinet

You'll eventually need a file cabinet to keep your published clips and other paraphernalia in, so buy at least one or two. You can store your materials in boxes, but your pets could jump on them, kids could spill things on them, and so forth. It is better if they are in a safe place away from prying eyes and sticky fingers.

(l) Lighting

Make sure that you have good lighting in your home office. As a writer you use your eyes constantly and you must avoid eye strain.

Lighting should be neither too dim nor too bright, and you must gauge what is best for you. You may wish to use adjustable lamps.

(m) Ergonomic devices

There are numerous devices to make your office better suited to your body and help you avoid such ailments as carpal tunnel syndrome, an ailment of the hands that can be exacerbated by too much typing.

For typing, get a copy holder. When you are typing information listed on papers, this device will enable you to see your copy at eye level without craning your neck.

You can also purchase telephone headsets to avoid straining your neck from balancing and cradling the phone between ear and shoulder. It is also easier to take notes this way.

Get a comfortable chair, preferably with arms, and be sure your back is well supported.

Remember, no matter how ergonomically balanced your office is, you should take periodic breaks and at least walk around the room. Don't stare intently at the computer screen for hours. You'll hurt your eyes. Instead, glance away periodically.

(n) Letterhead

Letterhead is essential when you are starting out and you need not spend a lot creating a gorgeous masterpiece, nor should you choose shocking pink or any other day-glo color for your paper. Use either white or off-white. If it is too fancy, it turns people off.

Keep your letterhead simple with your name, address, telephone number, and fax number. If you must, you can add professional affiliations, but mostly they don't enhance appearance. Don't put "freelance writer" or "writer" under your name. Tell the person you're a writer in the text of your letter.

Avoid pasting graphics and symbols all over your letterhead. Keep it simple. Use black ink. Colored ink costs more and is unlikely to net you any more sales.

I consider my letterhead even more essential than my fax machine, which I value highly. My sales went up dramatically after I created letterhead and I know I didn't become a better writer in just two weeks, especially since I was sending out the same ideas, written up the same way. The only difference was the letterhead.

Letterhead provides a feeling of professionalism, permanency, and seriousness.

You absolutely must use letterhead if you plan to be a profit-making writer.

You can ask a printer to assist you with designing your letterhead or you can design it yourself. I don't buy letterhead anymore. Instead, I have my letterhead template on disk, and when I want to type a letter, I call up that template. Then the whole document, letterhead and letter, is printed out on one pass through my laser printer. I use white copy paper.

(o) Business cards

Many writers consider business cards essential. Most of my work is done through telephone interviews. If you do in-person interviews, people expect you to have cards. They are an inexpensive investment. Forget the fancy stuff. Your name, address, telephone number, and fax number are sufficient.

(p) Brochures

Some writers create flyers or brochures with their photograph on the cover and listings of the type of work they do. This may be an option for you to consider once you have some experience under your belt.

(q) Reference books

Reference books are another valuable tool for every writer. A good college-level dictionary is essential and can be purchased from your local bookstore. I use *Merriam Webster's Collegiate Dictionary* in the paperback edition.

Another important reference is *Roget's International Thesaurus*. This source is extremely useful for those times when you don't want to use the same word twice or you can't quite think of the right word. If you draw a complete blank, you can page through the index and seek a similar word. I'm still using the 1979 edition, though you may prefer to use the most recent edition.

What about quotations? They can really make your prose sparkle. People have made wonderful remarks; a pithy quote may be just what you need to round out your article. The source I use for quotes is *The International Thesaurus of Quotations*.

A recent business reference that explains everything from "amortization" to "work-in process inventory" is *The Portable M.B.A. Desk Reference: An Essential Business Companion*, by Paul A. Argenti.

There are also specific reference books that outline major world events. If you want a quick and handy overview of history or cultural changes, books like the *Chronicle of the World* and *Chronicle of Canada* are also excellent.

(r) A camera

You don't have to be a professional photographer to use a camera. Writers are often in situations where pictures must be taken. Guess who gets to take them? You do!

Generally it is best to shoot color slides because you can get them developed locally. In addition, this is a format preferred by many periodicals. Some can also use color prints. Check with the editor first.

Black and white photos may be okay but it can be very hard to find a lab to develop them. If you can develop the photos yourself, fine, but this is certainly not a requirement.

I use a simple camera with auto-focus and auto-everything. I talk to my subject during the photo session (which is usually right after the interview), laugh, kid around, and don't shoot until the person looks at least marginally relaxed. Shoot a whole roll and you'll get at least one good photo in most cases.

Sometimes your interviewees have photos of themselves and they may have been professionally shot, which is good. But if you need a photo of your subject on the job or doing something, take those pictures yourself if you need to. Some writers take an introductory course on photography or read introductory books on the subject. Check your local community college and your library to see if these options are available to you.

(s) A tape recorder

I have one micro-cassette recorder to take out on interviews and one recorder hooked up to my phone to tape telephone interviews. No matter how effective you are at taking notes, often there are many distractions. People on the other end may be giving you complicated information. If you have it on tape, you can listen to it later and make sure you get it right.

Which is better, a micro-cassette recorder or a larger-sized recorder? I prefer the micro-cassette recorder for in-person interviews because it fits easily into a purse or briefcase and is quite unobtrusive and nonthreatening. The downside of micro-cassettes is that they are easy to lose, so be careful.

Whatever recorder you use, be sure to label your tapes. If you are interviewing many people for one article, several articles, or a book (or all of the above), it is too easy to become confused about which tape includes which interview. You don't want to waste your time listening to tapes over and over to find the right one.

Should you tape over tapes? That's a judgment call. When you have completed an interview and the project has been published, it is probably safe to tape over a month or two later, although some people save their tapes for years. If you do tape over a previous interview, be sure to relabel your tape.

To record over the telephone, you will need a recorder with a microphone input jack and a remote on/off jack. You can buy a simple device that allows you to easily hook up the recorder to the telephone line. Recorders are also available in many shops, but you may want to check out ones that specialize in audio equipment to find the best deal.

Tell the person that you are taping him or her at the beginning of the interview because you want your quotations to be accurate. Most people are terrified of being misquoted and appreciate being taped.

Important note: Take notes even when you are taping a person. For one thing, you can jot down thoughts as they occur to you without interrupting the flow of the interviewee's thoughts. Another reason is there are those horrible occasions when your tape machine runs out of tape and you don't realize it or it fails altogether. So take notes as an emergency backup.

(t) Calendar

Whether you buy a huge calendar to hang up on the wall or a desk-size calendar, you need to record your appointments, due dates, and other important information. Some people put this information on their computer, while others are happy to jot down the information on the appropriate date. If an upcoming interview is really important, I also annotate it a few days ahead of time. I also have been known to leave myself notes on the refrigerator!

Many writers swear by their office organizers, voluminous books containing telephone numbers, a calendar, and assorted other data.

3. Insurance

Insurance on your property is an issue that every writer intent on making a profit should consider. Many insurance companies offer plans that insure your computer and other expensive pieces of equipment for a fairly nominal fee.

You might think you should forego this. I'm glad I did not. Several years ago, a bolt of lightning shot through my telephone line into my modem and then into my turned-off computer, destroying it forever, including everything on the hard drive. Disasters like this are also a good argument for backing up your files. I had surge protection on my line, but this was a direct hit.

My insurance covered the full replacement cost of the computer — less a small deductible — and was well worth the small premium I had paid for it. I did, however, have to obtain a letter from the company that sold me the computer, attesting that lightning strikes can destroy a built-in modem.

4. Banking arrangements

Another point to consider is to set up a separate checking account for your business, although this is not necessary if you are doing business under your own name.

If you have an account in which you deposit business revenues and from which you draw on to pay business expenses, you will have a better general idea of how your business is doing than you would if you intermingled your family funds. You can still make personal withdrawals from the business, but when you do this, it is more noticeable than it would be if you had just one account.

* * *

Now that you know some basics, should you rush out and quit your job? Not so fast. Read the next chapter for a discussion on whether you should become a full- or part-time entrepreneurial writer and how you can make this decision.

3
PROPER PLANNING AND GOAL SETTING

a. SHOULD YOU QUIT YOUR DAY JOB?

Now that you know the basics of getting started, are aware of what tools are needed, and have mastered the writer's mind-set, should you go ahead and quit your job and become a rich and famous author, maybe in a few weeks? Well, not so fast.

First, it is important to understand that few writers become rich overnight. Why are most writing businesses not immediately profitable? Because you need time to build up your knowledge and experience, start your marketing, and develop a customer base.

b. WHEN SHOULD YOU QUIT YOUR DAY JOB?

To answer this question, you must consider many aspects of your own life. For example, do you have enough money saved to support yourself and your family? What if another family member who is now employed were laid off? Would you then still have adequate financial resources?

Keep in mind that your business will cost you dollars, primarily in overhead expenses. Even if you already own a computer, printer, and reams of paper, there will be expenses. Costs for computer disks, pens, phone expenses, etc. add up fast.

Also keep in mind that you may not receive payment for job until a month or more after you complete it. Let's say that you turn in your assigned cover story today. In 30 days (or maybe 60 days), the check finally arrives.

You should do a simple cash flow projection (see Sample #1). Please note, however, that your projection includes revenues and expenses to the business and does not cover what is essential to your daily life (i.e., food and shelter). You may wish to include these necessities in your cash flow budget.

Writing revenues are often very sporadic. You may receive a large check this week and then nothing for four weeks. You should have good budgeting skills and know how to s-t-r-e-t-c-h a paycheck, at least in the early part of your writing career.

c. PART-TIME WORK

You may wish to keep your day job and write part-time. One difficulty in working part-time is that if you're working on a piece that requires interviews, you need to keep in mind that most interviewees are only available during the day and that is when you are probably working outside your home.

It is not a great idea to use the boss's phone to call up and interview people for magazine articles you're supposed to be doing on your own time. And it could get you fired.

On the other hand, you can write queries in your spare time. There are many types of articles that you can write in your spare time — the personal experience piece, the personality profile, and, often, the how-to article.

It is also true that many interviewees will agree, and even prefer, to be interviewed during the evening or on the weekend. Away from day-time distractions, they are better able to concentrate on your questions.

CASH FLOW PROJECTION OVER FOUR MONTHS

CASH IN	Month 1	Month 2	Month 3	Month 4
Cash	0	$5,565	$5,425	$6,702
Savings	$8,000	0	0	0
Revenues	0	0	$1,500	$1,626
Total Cash	$8,000	$5,565	$6,925	$8,328
Expenses				
Postage	$35	$40	$40	$35
Telephone	$150	$100	$127	$200
Office Supplies	$250	0	$56	$77
Equipment	$2,000	0	0	0
Total Expenses	$2,435	$140	$223	$312
Cash Balance	$5,565	$5,425	$6,702	$8,016

d. WORKING FULL-TIME

When you decide to take the plunge and leave your full-time job for a full-time writing business, it can be very scary. But you'll be very motivated to succeed!

You should hit the ground running with a good plan for what you can write about, who you can write for, approximately how much revenue you anticipate receiving, and what your estimated costs will be. If you make such a plan *before* you quit your day job, you'll be ahead of the game and ahead of most writers.

Create a cash flow projection for yourself, taking into account cash, savings, and any other liquid (easily convertible to cash) assets you have now. To this amount, add in anticipated revenues and deduct anticipated expenses. This will give you an estimate of the cash you should have on hand for your business. The cash flow projection shown in Sample #1 includes only business expenses and no personal expenses. You may also wish to add in personal expenses as well.

e. AN EARNINGS PLAN

Talent alone isn't enough to lead you to success as an entrepreneurial writer. To be a profit-making writer, you need to plan how much money you want to make and how you are going to get it. This involves some hard thinking and serious goal setting.

Planning ahead can help you decide whether to write full-time or part-time. Making your own cash flow projection, like the one in Sample #1, is your first step to making an earnings plan.

Once you know what income you need, consider how much you (realistically) expect to make in one year: $10,000, $20,000, $50,000? Keep in mind that you must also cover your overhead expenses (adding at least 20% to your financial goal). Divide your desired annual earnings by 12 to calculate how much you need to earn per month. You may not know how much you can earn, but estimate to the best of your ability how much you need.

Set an annual goal and review it monthly to see where you stand. Be realistic. You're not going to make $100,000 in your first year as an entrepreneurial writer. If you're planning to work full-time, plan on earning a living wage. The premise of this is that with talent, aggressiveness, and good planning, you can make a living wage.

A sample earnings plan is provided in Sample #2. To avoid discouragement, don't set your goal so high that you can never succeed. If you find that your earnings are very low month after month, you can adjust your earnings goal downward. But don't be too easy on yourself.

f. SET MILESTONES

A milestone refers to a goal or series of goals that you have planned to complete by certain dates.

One problem many writers have is juggling many projects or even figuring out how to do one major project. I had 18 months to write a very lengthy and heavily researched book. It sounds like forever, but the time passes fast!

To avoid becoming overwhelmed, I recommend that you periodically create milestones. When a project is big (or you have many projects, or both), break down the project into smaller increments and into goals.

First, write down the tasks needed to perform each job. For example, for Job A you may need to identify five people to interview and then interview them, do some library and/or on-line research, and then write the article.

Let's say you have three weeks to do this job. You must then assign a portion of the time available to do each task. Don't leave the most time-consuming tasks until the last week.

SAMPLE #2
EARNINGS PLAN

Goal:	$30,000 gross sales per year, or $2,500/month		
	Received	Total Revenues	+/- Your Goal
JAN	$1,000	$1,000	-$1,500
FEB	4,000	5,000	0
MAR	2,000	7,000	-500
APR	3,200	10,200	+200
MAY	1,500	11,700	-800
JUNE	670	12,370	-2,630
JULY	2,100	14,470	-3,030
AUG	3,100	17,570	-2,430
SEPT	2,500	20,070	-2,430
OCT	2,476	22,546	-2,454
NOV	4,100	26,646	-854
DEC	4,378	31,024	+1024

You may have other assignments on the go as well. For Job B you already have done the research and interviewing and you need to sit down and write the article. This article is due in one week.

For Job C, you have written a first draft but you need to review it one more time. The article is due in two weeks.

Once you know what needs to be done to complete each assignment on time, you can make up a daily schedule. Each morning, write down a list of things you must do to achieve your daily goals.

After each task has been completed, you can check it off and feel very proud of yourself. See Sample #3 for a three-week plan and a list of daily tasks. Adapt it to your own needs.

As you move further into a project, you can become more specific. For example, you may identify Jane Brown and John Doe as people you must interview. Set weeks during which you'd like to interview them. Allow plenty of time because Jane and John may be on vacation, sick, or just too busy to talk to you when you want to talk to them.

I recommend posting your three-week plan on a bulletin board or wall or clipboard each so you can periodically remind yourself where you are on the project.

g. NUMBER OF PAGES

Depending on the length of the project, many writers set a goal for a certain number of pages to write each day. Set a goal that will stretch you but won't give you a nervous breakdown. Then give yourself a little reward when you're done. Go watch a favorite TV show, go for a walk, or just mellow out.

h. MARKETING GOALS

Many writers set a goal for the number of queries or proposals to send out per week. Maybe it's six, maybe it's ten. Set a goal that is reasonable for you, but make it more than one query per week. (Some writers routinely send out five to ten queries each week.)

If you are sending out many queries, you can track them on a simple form you create for this purpose (see Sample #4). You can also keep track of queries on a computer spreadsheet or database. Keep a copy of each query letter as well.

i. SET GOALS TO SAVE TIME

Time is money. Try to save as much time as possible. Sort the mail into piles of bills, junk, checks, etc. Throw out the mail you don't need. Deposit the checks today or no later than tomorrow to improve your financial position. Prioritize the action items that you identify among your mail.

For example, a client may have written with a question that needs a written reply. Decide how urgent it is to answer, but don't delay longer than a few days.

Make lists. To-do lists are good. You can also make lists of possible future ideas, lists of questions to ask interviewees, and a myriad of other lists.

Keep the papers and supplies you need nearby. If you have a project that is not due for months and you don't need to work on it now, file it away.

SAMPLE #3
THREE-WEEK PLAN

	Job A	Job B	Job C
Week 1	NEW JOB Goal: 5 interviews Library research Online research Networking Set up interviews	ONGOING JOB Write 1st draft Write final art	ONGOING JOB Rev. draft Call ed.
Week 2	Finish setting up interview Start interviewing Wrap up library research Wrap up online research		Write final
Week 3	Finish all research Write first draft Write final		

SAMPLE #4
TRACKING QUERIES AND SUBMISSIONS

Magazine Queries — June 199-

Market	Idea	Sent	Result
Markets Today	computer how-to	4/15	assignment due 7/15
Florida Armadillo	mating habits	5/25	rejected
Expo	Profile/Jane X	5/25	assignment due 6/30
Med. Payments	elec. billing	5/15	assignment due 7/10

4
GETTING ASSIGNMENTS

You've imbued yourself with the necessary writer's mind-set, you have the right equipment, and you're ready to start your writing career. How do you get ideas for topics to write about? And how do you get assignments once you find great ideas?

This chapter concentrates on generating ideas and finding places where you can sell them.

a. FINDING IDEAS TO WRITE ABOUT

There are so many things to write about if you only take the time to consider the possibilities. Many writers say that one lifetime is not long enough to explore every subject that interests them.

1. Read

Writers love to read. You need not concentrate on reading only culturally enlightening material — reading the latest bestsellers keeps you in tune with current language use and popular style. And it's fun too!

Read writers' magazines and newsletters. I have gleaned many leads from *Writing for Money*, (Blue Dolphin Communications, Wayland, Massachusetts) and *Freelance Writer's Report*, the newsletter published by Cassell Communications in North Sandwich, New Hampshire.

If you're interested in both fiction and non-fiction writing, also read *Writer's Digest*. If you prefer to write fiction, *The Writer* is a good monthly source. (See the Appendix for addresses.)

Check local newspapers. Perhaps a local club is running a special contest or a local resident has won recognition for a unique accomplishment. Is this something that has national appeal? Consider a national publication. Or a national club's publication. Would it interest business people? Hobbyists? Other markets?

2. Listen

Listen to your friends, relatives, and colleagues. What are they worried and concerned about? I wrote my first feature article back in 1981. At the time I lived in New Hampshire, which was about to be infested with the gypsy moth caterpillar. People were extremely upset about the impending tree holocaust. I knew this from listening to people at the post office, supermarket, and even my friends.

My query was accepted almost instantly. The article was quickly published and, although I resolved I'd never do another insect article again, I added a very good clip to my file.

3. Look at your own life

I wrote a how-to book on adoption after adopting a child. I have written many self-help or informative articles based on personal experiences. If it happened to you and you resolved a problem, you have the potential to help others — and get paid!

4. Watch a little television

I know this recommendation may sound somewhat heretical to many writers. It may well be a "vast wasteland," but there are many ideas that you can gain by watching (a limited amount of) television.

5. Get out

Join clubs, meet people, and network. The more you interact with others, the more you learn and the more ideas you can generate for possible writing assignments. In fact, you may write about some of the people you meet. Or they may hire you to write articles or reports for them.

6. Conferences

Go to writers' conferences when you can, particularly if the featured speakers are publishers, editors, or agents from New York or other big cities. Local conferences can also be fun, but if you can afford it, splurge on the conference in a city several hours away or even in another area so you can mix and mingle with potential customers from geographically diverse areas.

Often literary agents and editors attend and speak at writers' conferences. I was approached by an editor at a conference and asked if I could write an encyclopedia on adoption and come up with at least 100 different topics. By our breakfast meeting the next day I had 200 topics. *The Encyclopedia of Adoption* was published in 1991. This is an example of effective networking, a skill you must cultivate.

Sometimes others who attend conferences are actively seeking writers. A colleague of mine was approached by a woman who was seeking a ghost writer to write her life story. The two struck a deal at the conference.

Of course, writers' conferences don't always generate book or magazine assignments, but they usually offer sources of helpful information as well as tremendous enthusiasm for the writing field. Since most writers work alone, talking to others in the same field can be very fulfilling and encouraging.

Some seminars have opportunities for writers to sign up with agents or editors for individual conferences. Sign up and come prepared with several well-thought-out ideas.

b. FITTING IDEAS INTO NICHES

Optimize your research and time by using what you've already learned and build on that knowledge for future projects.

Does this mean you must specialize in one topic and work on it until the day you decide to retire or quit writing? Some people like to specialize in one area, but they generally also find many different niches within their specialty. For example, they may write only travel articles but consider themselves "generalists" because they write travel pieces for many different markets. Or perhaps they write health care articles but write them for both consumer and trade markets.

Then there are others, like me, who write about many different topics in totally unrelated fields. But I can build on what I have already learned in other markets, and so can you. After all, many great discoveries have been made by people not in the field. New entrants to a field bring fresh eyes and fresh perspectives.

What do you do with an idea when you have it? How do you know what market it is for? When you have a viable idea you should break it down into its various elements.

For example, I interviewed senior citizens in Florida who were helping the police by analyzing patterns of crime statistics. I wrote about them for a national retirement magazine, a Florida retirement magazine, a police magazine, and a retired officer magazine. (Two of the men I interviewed were retired from the military service.)

Each article was slanted or targeted to the readers of that particular publication. Yet my basic research covered me for all of them; the only extra work I had to do was make one or two quick phone calls to add a little extra information.

Each article was unique and special and each market gained a good story. I maximized my work and increased my revenues.

Sometimes you can sell an article you have written with no changes at all, which is nice. If you have sold one-time or first rights only to a publication, then you have the right to turn around and sell your article to another company after your article is published.

I have sold and re-sold articles with no changes whatsoever. The checks aren't usually huge — but it's nice to receive $50 or $100 for virtually no effort or expense, other than the letter I sent. I usually photocopy the entire piece so that it is very obvious to the prospective client that it has already been published.

In another case, I wrote about a woman who sold teddy bears through the mail. I wrote about her for an entrepreneurial magazine, a Boston business publication, a woman's publication, and a teddy bear trade magazine. I could have continued writing about her, but other topics captured my attention.

You can also write about people based on their ethnic background, gender, age, club membership, religion, area they live in, or career; these are just a few categorical breakdowns.

So when you do have an idea, consider all its possible elements before you pitch it any particular magazine. You may be able to sell your article — rewritten or sometimes as a reprint — to many different markets and get a good return on the time and money you've expended.

Often your clips on one job enable you to win a job in a related field, even if you know nothing about it.

The level of research and the quotations you have used are taken carefully into account by the editor or prospective client. I recommend sending different samples to show your diversity.

For example, I used a lengthy report I wrote on "repetitive strain injuries" to obtain contracts for writing about health care topics. The editors presumed I had some basic knowledge as well as the capacity to learn because they had spoken to me on the phone and they had reviewed my clips.

I have also written about the business end of health care, based on the fact that I have many business clips and have earned an M.B.A.

Brainstorm. Make a list of what you are knowledgeable and curious about and see if there are any crossovers.

Spinning off ideas and categories of ideas is a very good way to maximize your writing revenues.

c. NETWORKING

Although your fellow writers are also potential competitors, they may have opportunities they can share or jobs they don't want or don't need.

When you are offered a job that isn't suitable or doesn't interest you, why not offer it to a fellow writer? I have, and payback time eventually comes around when your fellow writer offers you a chance at an interesting job.

It may be hard to network with fellow writers because many are rather individualistic. But you can meet other writers at clubs or on on-line computer forums, such as the Journalism Forum (JForum) or Literary Forum (LitForum) on CompuServe.

d. FIGURING OUT WHERE THE MARKETS ARE

If you're interested in the magazine market, you should obtain a copy of *The Writer's Market*, a book which is published by Writer's Digest, Inc. each autumn.

This resource describes consumer and trade magazines, what types of articles they most want, what types they DON'T want, and how much they pay. It also includes information on book publishers.

e. STUDY THE PUBLICATION YOU WANT TO WRITE FOR

If you have an idea that you think would fit a particular magazine, read over at least one copy of the publication to see if you're on target. Sometimes the title of the magazine may sound very different from what the subject matter covers, and editors consistently report that their pet peeve is being queried with off-the-wall ideas that don't begin to fill their needs. Don't make this mistake!

As you read a magazine, look at the content and style of the articles. Do the writers use a lot of quotations? Are the articles heavily anecdotal? Get a "feel" for the publication.

Be sure to read the "Letters to the Editor" section because this part of a magazine shows you what the readers like — and don't like — about the magazine, and also what the editors thought important enough to print.

Look at the column written by the editor or publisher, if there is one. Often he or she highlights key areas of concern and this section is important because it may generate ideas.

Look at the ads. If this periodical is full of ads to help you stay younger, rid your face of wrinkles, and help you exercise, and there's little mention of children or parenting, it would probably not be a good idea to suggest a be-a-better-parent article to the editor.

On the other hand, if the magazine is full of ads for baby products, your idea on how to cope with the all-night new baby blues could be of interest.

Incidentally, you don't have to order or buy all the magazines you may wish to write for. Every time I visit the doctor or dentist, I quickly thumb through every magazine. And yes, I have found markets for my work.

5
MARKETING IS THE KEY TO SUCCESS

You have a great book contract or maybe six magazine articles lined up. Or both! You're on your way, and won't have to worry any more about getting jobs, right?

Wrong! The successful writer never forgets the importance of marketing, which refers to actively selling your ideas to prospective clients. Editors leave, magazines fail, and publishing houses are sold, merged, or fold. Business people retire and clients move on. As a result, it is very wise to spend at least 20% to 30% of your time working on obtaining more work — from your old customers as well as new ones.

Yet when you have plenty of work to do, it is natural to concentrate just on doing that work and forgetting about next month or next year. Don't make this serious mistake.

Marketing is important because you never win all the jobs you bid on. No matter how rhapsodic a client may be about your work, he or she may be unable or unwilling to hire you.

a. TARGETING YOUR MARKET

Before you send out query letters or manuscripts, understand who it is you are writing to and why this editor or publisher or client may be interested in your idea.

Dana Cassell, publisher of *Freelance Writer's Report*, says "many writers have an idea and think that everybody wants to know about it, so they shotgun it out there. But different magazines have different readers and different demographics."

b. QUERY LETTERS: MINI-PROPOSALS

A query letter is usually a one-page letter to convince the editor to hire you to write about what you're describing. If it is a query for a magazine article, you either get the go-ahead or a rejection to write the piece, although sometimes more information is requested.

Sometimes you get no reply at all. Follow up after a month or so if you still want to do the piece. I have had editors contact me over a year after I submitted queries to them! One told me he found my query after he moved the file cabinet and asked if I still wanted to write the book. In that case, I did not.

If it is a query for a book you want to write, an interested editor or agent usually asks you for a book proposal and a few sample chapters.

Here are some basic elements you should be sure to incorporate into your one-page, single-spaced letter:

(a) Start with a fact, anecdote, or interesting statistic. It should be something that will capture the a reader's interest and inspire him or her to read on.

(b) Explain in one or two paragraphs what you want to write about and why readers of this publication would be interested. Do you want to research and write about an endangered species, an illustrious businessperson, or some other topic?

(c) Give your slant or hook. The slant is the underlying angle or thesis of your article. For example, is the sea life in your area being killed or injured by boaters? Is the recent layoff at a large plant going to drastically affect the local economy? Or perhaps your slant is one of national scope. For example, you see a trend toward older Americans returning to work. Sell the angle that you'd like to pursue.

(d) If you have any clips, tell the editor you'd be happy to forward them if he or she is interested. If you don't have any clips, do *not* say you are a novice writer.

(e) If you have credentials that might be relevant, then say so. For example, if you have an M.B.A. and you want to sell your idea to a business publication, mention it. Your Ph.D. in anthropology, however, is best left out.

(f) Tell the editor how many words you want to write. There are about 250 words on a double-spaced typewritten page. If the word count you offer is too much or too little but he or she still wants the article, the editor can tell you how much to write.

(g) To SASE or not to SASE? Many writers' publications routinely advise new writers to always enclose a self-addressed stamped envelope with your query. I violate this rule constantly. If the editor is interested enough in my idea, he or she will spend the postage to tell me so. And if not, I'll probably receive a form letter or short note. Why should I pay to receive a rejection letter? Professionals and business people are expected to answer their mail.

If you do send an SASE with your letter, I recommend that you send only your query and not a ream of clips to go with it. Imagine how much postage that will cost to return! Instead, tell the editor that you will provide samples of your writing if needed. If you don't have any samples, say nothing.

(h) Next, sell yourself: abandon your modesty. (Don't be arrogant, of course, and never lie!) If you don't have any credits in this area, do *not* say so. It's a major mistake to refer to what you don't have.

Instead, allude to your positive attributes or accomplishments that relate to the story you want to write. For example, you're an active environmentalist and won a "green" award last year, so you'd be right for that recycling piece. Or you've written over 20 personality profiles on business people and thus you're the right one to profile a celebrity for a popular magazine.

Also, be sure to refer to personal strengths. For example, I make it a point to tell every editor that I meet deadlines. (Be honest!) Or perhaps you are an excellent and rapid researcher.

(i) Some writers include their resume in query letters. I keep one on file but I am rarely asked for it. Instead, I am asked for samples of my work. If the client likes my work and wants to hire me, he or she doesn't care about my academic credentials or what I did right after graduating from college.

Make a copy of your query. It would be very embarrassing if an editor called and asked you to write about something you forgot about submitting. This happened to me once a very long time ago. I never made that mistake again.

After you send out your query, start working on your next one! Do not sit and wait to receive an assignment. You should have at least three to four queries (preferably more) out at any one time in order to maintain a steady work flow. Inevitably, some of your great ideas will be rejected, but when you still have several ideas out there, a rejection is much less painful.

See Samples #5 and #6 at the end of this chapter for two examples of query letters. Adapt the query letter to suit your style. Try to write compellingly and let your enthusiasm shine through.

c. TELEPHONE QUERIES

Some writers believe that calling up an editor, publisher, or other person to pitch an idea is the height of tackiness. I disagree. You may have a wonderful idea that is very timely and you don't want to wait to convey your idea to the person who needs it.

You could fax your queries, but unsolicited faxes annoy many people. I recommend using the telephone.

If you're going to talk to someone you already know, your telephone query should be relatively easy. Prepare your basic idea anyway. Be prepared to talk about your slant, when you can do it, how long you think it should be, etc.

But if you are calling a total stranger on a cold call, write down a few notes ahead of time. Psych yourself up and put on your best "smiley face" voice and think of yourself as a runner crashing through the tape at the finish line.

When you call, be certain to ask if this is a convenient time. He or she may be rushing to meet a deadline or puzzling over some very confusing data. If so, ask if you may call back. In most cases, the answer is yes.

I like telephone queries because the editor expresses reservations or concerns about my topic and I can counteract them immediately. Maybe he or she is worried that the subject won't appeal to baby boomers, for example, so you can point out that baby boomers are concerned about this topic. The editor may say that he or she might want this topic in a few months. Ask if you can call back then.

One thing to keep in mind is that the more the other person talks and the more you listen, the more likely it is that you'll make a sale. This technique works far better than the talk-only mode employed by too many people who sell products. The editor or publisher wants to know that his or her special needs are being taken into account. Listen carefully to find out what those needs are. If you are too busy talking about your own goals and expect the editor to listen to you, he or she will quickly tune you out.

Actively listen to the other person's expressed needs, then explain how your article, book, or pamphlet can solve the problem, and use the other person's own words and phrases.

Most people are used to others NOT listening to them. People truly wish to be heard and if you are one of those rare people who can listen and also respond, then you will be considered a valuable asset.

Sometimes when you make a telephone or written query, the editor may not be interested in the idea you're pitching, but he or she may have a different and perhaps even more compelling idea he or she would like to offer you as an assignment. Listen and consider it! This could be your opportunity to break into this market.

However, don't say yes right away, no matter how much you want to! Find out what the alternative idea is and think about whether you would like to do it or not. They don't give the easy ones to unknown writers — you're more likely to get a tough job that the editor doesn't have time to do or doesn't know how to do, or both.

d. ON-LINE MARKETING

One fairly new method of marketing yourself and landing assignments is through computer networks like CompuServe, GEnie, Prodigy, the Internet, and a myriad of others.

These are for-profit services that enable people worldwide to communicate with each other through the use of a personal computer, a modem, and a telephone. (See the Appendix for a list of several major on-line services.)

I have obtained many assignments through CompuServe, merely by responding to messages on the Journalism Forum or the Literary Forum. There is a certain camaraderie to on-line databases and less formality than querying by mail or even by a cold call. This does not, however, mean there are never any problems with on-line assignments.

As with all your jobs, you should be careful. Ask questions. If the individual is launching a new magazine and wants to pay you later, shy away. Later may never come — the magazine may fold before he or she pays you. Certainly you should always ask for a significant up-front payment: at least one-third of the entire job.

On the other hand, if you are careful and keep your eyes open, you can spot many good opportunities. I wrote profiles for a trade magazine for several years based on a message from a new publisher who left word on CompuServe that he was looking for a business writer.

I have also written for large corporations through contacts on CompuServe. And I have identified good opportunities on America Online as well.

The "trick" to successful networking on-line, as well as in your personal contacts with others in the field off-line, is to sometimes give information and leads without expecting anything in return.

Trading information can be a very powerful way to succeed in life.

Trading information with others is a valuable technique that can work for you. If you learn that someone is actively seeking information or some resource that you are aware of, give the other person the information.

This doesn't mean you spend all your time seeking lost souls who need help. However, when you can readily supply information, even though there is no immediate or obvious gain to you, it is a good idea to do it.

You will eventually find that because you have helped people in the past, people are more likely to respond to your requests for help and information. This doesn't mean that everyone owes you because you passed on information. What happens instead is that you create an atmosphere of sharing by your willingness to provide information, and this makes people more likely to help you when you need information.

e. LITERARY AGENTS

You may decide to leave the marketing to others by hiring an agent. There are both good and bad literary agents. It is unwise to immediately sign up with an agent just because he or she is willing to take you on.

Most literary agents work with book writers, not magazine writers, because they generally charge 15%, and 15% of $5,000 is much better than 15% of $500. A good agent will shop your book proposal around to major publishers after providing you with some basic advice on how to improve your proposal. Don't expect your agent to write the proposal for you.

I think the best reference guide for literary agents is the *Insider's Guide to Book Editors, Publishers, and Literary Agents* by Jeff Herman. It is published by Prima Publishing with a new edition every year. (See the

Appendix for further information.) This book lists agencies and addresses and provides the names and interests of particular agents and books they have sold in the past. As a result, you may be able to match your interests with prospects in this book.

Many publishers refuse to look at unsolicited queries or proposals, so getting a contract with a major publisher on your own is unlikely. Success is certainly not guaranteed with an agent, but the odds are much improved.

One point that I think is important to keep in mind is that even though the agent is *your* agent, most are really concerned with pleasing the publishers — the ones with the money. The agent wants to have a continuing and happy relationship with major publishers. So don't presume that all agents are concerned with your interests solely. That would be naive.

This does not mean you should never consider hiring a literary agent. Agents can open important doors for you. Contracts with agents vary greatly and if you can, you should try to get a per-book contract. If you sign a time-limited contract, try to limit the time period to no more than one year.

Most agents don't charge for phone calls, photocopies, and reading manuscripts, but some do. Find out how an agent you are considering handles extra charges.

When you are offered a contract from a publisher, your agent reviews it and lets you decide whether to accept or turn down the offer. The agent then forwards the contract to you for signing. Often he or she will negotiate changes with the publisher first on your behalf.

When the check for the advance comes, it usually goes to your agent. This seems strange to most people, including me, but there is a lot about publishing that is rather strange.

He or she cashes the check, keeping his or her agreed-upon percentage. The agent then remits a check for the balance to you. He or she should turn around your money within a week or two of receiving it.

If you earn back your entire advance and the royalties keep coming in, your agent receives those checks, deducts his or her cut and then sends on the balance to you. He or she also receives royalty statements and then forwards them to you.

If you decide to end your relationship with your agent, he or she usually continues to collect royalties and forward the checks to you.

As you can probably see, your agent must be a person you feel you can trust and have a good working relationship with. He or she need not be your best friend, but there should be a certain camaraderie there.

Should you hire an agent? This is a question too individual and too difficult to explore in this book. Many people are very successful without agents while others swear they would be nowhere had it not been for the valuable assistance of their agent.

I recommend you attend writers' conferences, meet agents, read books about literary agents, and carefully consider the pros and cons for your own individual situation before signing on with anyone. For example, if an agent handles mostly fiction (i.e., 70% of the agent's clients write fiction), and you are a non-fiction writer, why would you sign with this person? Go with someone who concentrates on non-fiction unless you have a really good reason for signing on with the fiction expert.

f. SELF-PUBLISHING

If you choose to do your own publishing, whether it's a newsletter, a booklet, or a book, you need to market the product. In fact, the time to start selling is before your newsletter or book is launched so you can raise some capital to get it going.

I publish a monthly newsletter on adoption and sell it to under 1,000 customers.

My list of customers was primarily derived through responses to direct-mail postcards. I used a list of people I developed myself and bought lists from several other specialized sources such as the newsletter, *The Adopted Child*, and from organizations such as the National Adoption Information Clearinghouse in Rockville, Maryland, and Tapestry Books (a company that concentrates on selling adoption books by many different publishers) in Ringoes, New Jersey.

I also reviewed magazines such as *OURS* (now called *Adoptive Families*) for articles and organizations and individuals whose addresses were published and who might be interested in my newsletter.

In addition, I actively solicited names from contacts in the field that I had discovered when I researched my book.

Finally, I searched on-line telephone databases on CompuServe. I used *adoption* as a keyword in my search of the Yellow Pages index and located the names of new

adoption agencies. You can also purchase such information on CD-ROMs.

g. VANITY PRESSES

A vanity press is a publisher who will publish your book for a fee. Be careful of vanity presses that make grandiose promises; they usually can't and don't deliver. They make their money from your money, rather than by selling your book. If your book sells any copies at all, it is most likely to be copies that you sell.

Sometimes a vanity publisher may work out well for you. For example, let's say you're a businessperson who needs a brochure or pamphlet and you need minor editing. There are legitimate enterprises that can take your project from a rough draft to a final product. Always be cautious, however; it is your money.

The ins and outs of bookselling for the self-publisher are complex. If you are interested in self-publishing, there are some very helpful books listed in the Appendix.

SAMPLE #5
QUERY LETTER FOR A PROFILE

July 29, 199-

Mary Alice Teddy
Teddies Forever
999 Maple Lane Road
Wonderful, NJ 00000

Dear Ms. Teddy:

Most people have books on their bookshelves, but Fran Lewis has collectible teddy bears on display in her living room bookcase. She has bears sitting in the living room, bears in the bedrooms, and bears in the bathroom.

Lewis is known as the "Bear Lady" in Concord, Massachusetts. Not only does she love bears, but she also sells them to fellow bear lovers worldwide. She has even hired bear designers to create unique bears for her mail-order catalogue.

I'm a freelance writer with many credits for writing profiles. (Several of my clips are enclosed.) I'd like to write a profile of Lewis, the Bear Lady, for your publication; I'm offering 1,500 words. My slant will be how bears dominate Lewis's business and personal life.

Thank you.

Christine Adamec

July 29, 199-

Ms. Sally Nofrills
Business Only
5555 Elm Tree Lane
Toronto, Ontario
Z1P 0G6

Dear Ms. Nofrills:

Fran Lewis will earn just under $1 million this year selling teddy bears by mail. Sound frivolous? She's a tough businesswoman who wouldn't end her business when her husband walked out, her partner quit, and the bank called in her loan.

"I never give up," she said. And she doesn't.

Today, Lewis sells a variety of teddy bears to adult collectors throughout the United States, both by catalogue and in her retail business. She plans to expand the business as well, taking on additional staff and products.

I'm a business writer who would like to write a business profile for you on Lewis, the "Bear Lady" of Concord, Massachusetts. I've written numerous business pieces in the past and several clips are enclosed. I have an M.B.A. and I meet deadlines.

Does 2,000 words plus photos sound like it might fit your needs?

Thank you.

Christine Adamec

6
DIFFERENT MARKETS, COAUTHORING, AND GHOSTWRITING

Many writers launch their writing careers with magazine features, while others start by writing books. Feature writers may then move to writing a book while authors may decide to write for trade or consumer publications or write for businesses. Most successful writers juggle a variety of writing projects.

There are also many opportunities to write for corporations, newsletter publishers, and many options in ghostwriting. In some cases, you may be hired to take over a job that another writer could not complete, and this chapter discusses the pros and cons of such an undertaking.

Perhaps you may be considering coauthoring a project with another person. The potential joys and pitfalls of such an undertaking are also covered in this chapter.

a. CATEGORIES/GENRES FOR BOOKS AND MAGAZINE WRITING

1. The personality profile (or biography)

People love to read about other people, whether it is the elusive Michael Jackson or an average person who survived a difficult crisis.

The personality profile is a wonderful genre for the novice or the experienced freelancer. Fascinating people always live in your community and thousands of miles away.

I recently profiled the Canadian regional manager of the Toronto-based National Marine Manufacturers Association, although I live in Florida. Using my interviewing skills over the phone, I obtained information my readers and trade show managers would love.

I have also interviewed many people in my own city, including an amateur radio expert who discussed an upcoming conference, a 70-year-old woman who just received her bachelor's degree in social work and is planning on becoming a social worker, a successful insurance saleswoman who was on welfare ten years ago, and many more.

Newspapers, trade magazines, and general interest magazines are starved for good personality profiles. They all know that people like to read about people for inspiration. The family that tirelessly works with a disabled child inspires other families whose children suffer from similar disabilities. The formerly dirt-poor woman who is now a wealthy salesperson probably has some good secrets and advice to share.

Personality profiles also provide entertainment, information, and juicy gossip. The personality profile is frequently a very favorable piece, although in some cases, it is neutral or even negative.

2. The how-to

The how-to book or article offers practical advice to the reader on how to achieve some goal: how to program a computer, put up wallpaper, or become a writer.

In this genre, the writer needs to provide details that a reader can follow, a kind of blueprint for success. How-to books or articles are extremely popular and there are many opportunities in this field.

Think about what you and your friends or colleagues already know about and what someone, somewhere might find valuable. My very first article back in 1981 was on how to plan a party. I hadn't planned a party in years — but my friends had, so I obtained practical and immediately usable information from them and wrote that article and many more for the editor.

3. The exposé

This type of article or book can be tough and is certainly not for the faint-of-heart. In the exposé you describe some beliefs, statements, or actions of someone and expose the flaws. There are plenty of bad people, crimes, and problem areas out there to write about if taking on tough issues appeals to you.

4. General information

Many articles or books provide general introductory information for readers who have interest in a topic but don't want to rush out and achieve whatever the writer or interviewees have done. What these readers want is an overview of the field.

5. Entertainment

In the entertainment genre, you amuse and/or entertain your readers. Often this genre is combined with others. For example, you may profile a public figure in an entertaining way. Often general information written in a light and easy style falls under this genre.

6. Editorial/op-eds

In these pieces, the writer takes a stand on an issue and presents the evidence for his or her views in an attempt to refute the opposition. People read editorials because they too have a strong position on the issue that may or make not correspond with yours.

7. The round-up

A round-up article involves asking many people the same question and is popular in columns as well as magazine and newspaper articles. Often the people who are asked the question are celebrities. They may have little or no expertise on whatever is asked, but because they are famous what they say will interest readers.

8. Personal experience

This can be a humorous little piece or can be a bare-your-soul article or book. The common denominator of the personal experience piece is that the writer has experienced a problem or knows someone else who has. (For example, some authors excel at "as-told-to" stories.) Often such a piece is written to educate and help the readers.

9. Problem solver

Related to the personal experience piece is what I call the professional "problem solver." You research and write about a problem faced in a field or profession and discuss how others have solved it. These articles are very much in demand and always will be. Generally, they revolve around how a business can get more customers, make more money, save time, and cope with competition. The problems are common to all businesses, and articles that give solutions will always interest people.

Many articles or books combine elements of different genres. For example, the personality profile can be a light, feel-good piece that makes its subject want to enshrine it over his or her mantel, or it may be a more balanced piece that shows its subject's flaws.

b. GETTING INTO MAGAZINES

Okay, let's say you want to launch your career by writing for magazines, which can be very lucrative if you succeed. What are the basics you need to know? To start with, you need to learn how to write a query letter describing your idea. It is vitally important that your letter get the attention of the magazine feature editor.

How do you know who to send the letter to? You check *Writer's Market, Writer's Digest, Writing for Money,* and other publications and find the name of an editor. Never ever send the letter blindly to "The Editor."

You could also check the masthead of a recent edition of the magazine you're interested in writing for. The masthead is usually near the front of the magazine and it lists the editorial staff. The masthead will also give you the correct title of each person's position and the mailing address and telephone number of the magazine. It may sound silly, but an editor-in-chief does not wish to be called a mere editor. So get that title right too. Also, double check the spelling of the person's name — this is very important.

Once you receive some interest and negotiate a reasonable fee, you can get started with your research and writing. Here are some basic tips for magazine feature writing:

(a) Find out the number of words the editor wants and avoid exceeding it. It is usually okay if the editor says a feature should be 2,000 words and your final product is 2,100, but don't submit 3,000 words. Edit it down.

(b) Emulate the style of the magazine. If it uses quotations, you should use them. If the magazine uses statistics, try to find some. You don't have to take on the persona of previous writers, but the tone of your writing should complement and fit in with the magazine's style.

Examine the writing style of the publication. What sort of words are used? Are the articles expressed in simple language or are they comprised of long sentences and multisyllabic words?

(c) Many magazine editors love sidebars (i.e., boxes of text placed within an article). A sidebar can be a chart, a graph, or a bullet-list of your major points. If you can think of anything that might fit into a sidebar format, be sure to tell the editor.

(d) You don't always have to start at the bottom of the pay scale. Many writers have recommended that in magazine writing, you start with the lowest-paying market as a new writer and slowly work your way up. I don't understand this advice at all. Instead, I recommend starting with the highest-paying market and working your way down.

Just because you're new doesn't mean major publishers will automatically turn you down. If you have a very good idea, you have a chance at getting the go-ahead. Of course, higher-paying publications are harder to get a yes from.

c. WRITING NEWSLETTER ARTICLES

Because of desktop publishing, newsletters are springing up everywhere. And newsletter editors need copy. Many of them will beg for free information. Others are willing to pay for good copy.

Often, writing for the newsletter is just another chore to the staff; this works to your advantage. A newsletter can represent steady income for the entrepreneurial writer who may be offered the chance to write some or even all of the material.

Once your client is happy with your work and trusts you, you are a necessary part of his or her overall plan whether the editor realizes this or not.

Newsletter publishers like to contract out work because it is cost-effective — no benefits, no vacation pay, and so forth.

Generally, newsletter articles are tightly written in a style similar to a newspaper piece. The difference is that your copy is highly targeted to the interests of the readers, whether they are adoptive parents, train collectors, or physicians in group practice.

d. WRITING BOOKS

If you have an idea you'd like to cover in much greater length than possible in a magazine feature, and your idea will appeal to at least several thousand buyers, then maybe you should write a book. First, write a query letter to editors and agents who you think might be interested in your book idea.

Note: Before you do your research and write up an entire manuscript, you need to prepare a book proposal. A book proposal can be ten pages or 50 or more pages; it is a complete description of what you want to do and why it should be done.

Do *not* send your entire proposal out unsolicited. It is too expensive and is the mark of an amateur. Instead, first send out your one-page letter written to pique the interest of an editor or agent. Also state that your book proposal is available. Then, if you are asked for your proposal, send it.

Print out a neat new copy and place it inside a plain pocket folder. Clip your cover letter stating that you are responding to the person's request to the outside of the pocket folder.

There are several sources on how to write book proposals but basically a proposal addresses these concerns:

(a) Why the book should be written.

(b) Who will want to read it. Include as much information as possible about your prospective readers, e.g., profession, socioeconomic status, gender, etc. Never say that everyone in the world will want to read your book because they won't.

(c) What the competition is like. There is almost always at least one competing book. Describe how your book is different and why it is better. Go to the library and review *Books in Print* under the subject category to find books similar to the book you want to write. Then find those books and scan them.

You don't necessarily have to buy these books. Tell your reference librarian you are a writer and ask if he or she can borrow them through an inter-library loan. Or go to a local college library and see if the books are there. Review them quickly and take notes.

(d) A description of what your book will cover and an annotated chapter listing.

(e) A discussion of the research you plan to do. Will you interview 100 people or only the foremost expert on your topic? If people in the field have already agreed to be interviewed by you, be sure to name them, their titles, and level of expertise.

(f) Why you should write this book. Aside from the passion you have for your topic (and don't leave that aspect out!), why are you the right person to write this book? Is it because you are an expert in the field? Or because you are an excellent researcher?

Provide as many reasons as you can think of, both emotional and practical, on why you should author this proposed book.

(g) Information about your background and interest in the subject. This is like a resume but in narrative form. Write about yourself in the third person as if someone else was writing about you. Don't be modest but don't make ridiculous claims to expertise that you do not have.

(h) Sample chapters. Many times, editors and/or agents request one or two sample chapters of your proposed book as a necessary part of your proposal.

You need not submit the first two chapters, but you probably don't want to submit the introduction and the conclusion, and nothing else. Instead, submit two well-written chapters that represent your best work.

e. WRITING FOR CORPORATIONS

Many businesses need writers but they are also afraid to try untested people. So often if you are given the go-ahead by a business, large or small, you'll be told that this is a "test" or a "trial." This is okay. Do a good job and you'll be asked to do more work.

Corporations need press releases, newsletter copy, annual reports, and a wide array of written material. Contact the public relations department of a large corporation or the president of a small company to learn about a company's writing needs. Be prepared to submit samples of your work.

f. BEING A GHOSTWRITER

Some writers say they could never ever ghostwrite because they must have their names on everything they write. They don't work just for money, but also for recognition. If seeing your name in print is important to you, then you might consider part-time ghostwriting, where you would see your name some or most of the time.

But if you can't bear the thought of not having a byline, or even worse, seeing another's name on your golden words, don't be a ghostwriter.

Politicians, teachers, physicians, and people from all walks of life hire ghostwriters. In many cases, they may be very competent at writing, but don't have the time to research or write a piece. In other cases, they are not competent writers and want to hire you to translate their thoughts into something coherent and interesting.

Many books by famous personalities are actually written by ghostwriters for hefty fees. Ghostwriters are also used by trade magazines, professional newsletters, and other publications.

How do you find clients? Some people advertise for ghostwriters in writers' publications. However, more frequently ghostwriters find their clients through networking. Get the word out that you can and will do ghostwriting. Tell editors, publishers, and colleagues in the field.

On the plus side, there are many people who will pay writers to write for them, whether it is a personal story, family history, adventure, or other type of book or article. The market is wide open.

On the negative side, if you ghostwrite for an individual as opposed to a company or corporation, you will usually find that the person has a very strong emotional attachment to his or her story. Often he or she may perceive it as the achievement of a lifetime.

As a result, the individual who hires you can be very emotional about his or her book, and if you are not careful, he or she can intrude on your personal life or make unreasonable demands. If your client calls you in the evenings to talk about the book, gently tell the client that this is unprofessional and insist that he or she stop. Neither is it your job to find a publisher for the finished manuscript.

You must have a contract that clearly sets out all terms and conditions. You also need to set ground rules for your client. Even if you think the story has great commercial potential, don't guarantee publication.

You may write a wonderful book that your client decides to rewrite. If you've promised that the book will be published, you will regret that promise.

Even if your client is a joy to work with and the story is fascinating, the most you should promise is to write the book or article and offer one free rewrite. But if you wish to go one step beyond and provide some assistance in marketing, be sure to add that on to the fee you've negotiated.

What if your client accepts your ghost-written manuscript and pays you and then an editor expresses interest in the manuscript but wants some rewriting? If the client accepted your work and paid you, then the job is done. If he or she wants more work to be done, then you should charge more money — if you are willing to take on the task.

Another problem with working for individuals as opposed to corporations is that individuals often plead poverty and beg you to give them the lowest rate possible. It is understandable that they should try this tactic — but don't fall for it.

If a client can't afford your fees, which should be fair, based on the terms and conditions needed to complete the job, then he or she should hire someone else.

Sample #7 is a checklist outlining some key questions you should ask yourself and your client every time you consider a ghost-writing project. Prepare your own checklist and adapt the questions to address your own unique concerns and needs.

The questions in Sample #7 may make being a ghostwriter sound like a very daunting and fearsome task. While this isn't always the case, it is important to ask the tough questions right away to avoid problems later on.

Many people will ask you to write their book on speculation and, later on when the book is a bestseller, they will split the profits with you. Consider an offer like this carefully before you accept. You are going to do all the work, take all the risk, and then share the profits — which may come years later. Don't do it. Instead, ask for enough money so that you can make a profit. And

also ask for a percentage of the royalties in the event that the book *is* sold and *does* become a bestseller.

g. TAKING OVER JOBS FROM OTHER WRITERS

One good opportunity that many writers are unaware of is the chance to take over a job dropped by another writer.

The writer may have dropped out of the job because he or she was sick, was daunted by the topic, couldn't make the deadline, or for other reasons.

If you are thinking about taking over a job from another writer, realize the editor or client is very frustrated and possibly even panicked. How is he or she going to meet that deadline? Often you will not be given very much time to complete a project.

Scope out the job and see what has already been done. You may be able to use some of the work the previous writer did or you may have to scrap everything and start from scratch. Ask to see any research materials from the previous writer if available *before* you cost out the job.

Also, ask to be paid up-front: as much as one-third of the total fee to be paid in advance. Be sure to ask for phone and fax expenses as well as travel expenses if they are needed. Write your own outline of what is needed for the project and clear it with the customer before you begin serious work.

h. COAUTHORING A PROJECT

Let's say you and your best friend or someone else you admire want to team up and write a book. What a great idea, right? You get along, you know each other, so you won't need a contract.

Wrong. If you expect your book to make any money (and if you don't, why write it?) and if you would also like to keep your relationship intact, then you need a contract.

Spell out what you are supposed to do and what your coauthor is supposed to do

CHECKLIST FOR POTENTIAL GHOSTWRITING CLIENTS

a. QUESTIONS TO ASK YOURSELF

1. Do I understand what this person wants and can I do it?

2. Do I have enough time to take on this project?

3. How will I feel if and when this book or project is published and my client gets all the glory? Can my ego take that?

4. Am I strong enough to stand up to this client if we have a problem?

b. QUESTIONS TO ASK THE POTENTIAL CLIENT

1. What is his or her true agenda in hiring you to do this work? Is it because he or she is not a good writer and/or lacks confidence? Or does he or she not have enough time?

2. What hidden agendas are there? Does the client seek fame and fortune or, in some cases, does he or she want to right a perceived wrong?

3. Will the client listen to your advice? (This is a tough one because everyone is on their best behavior at first.) Where can you see potential problems?

4. What is it that the client expects from you? Don't assume it is merely writing the book. It may also be selling the book to an agent or publisher, doing innumerable rewrites, and answering all questions or concerns that come up. How much does he or she want to take and how much are you willing to give?

5. Do you think you can get along with this client? No matter how many dollars he or she is waving in your face, if your gut instinct screams out no, you should listen.

and when. It should also be clear how any profits will be divided.

If the work is an even 50/50 split, then you may each be happy taking half. But often one person does more work than the other. Decide up front who does what. For example, you may be great at interviewing and your coauthor may be an excellent writer who hates research. Perhaps you are good at first drafts and he or she is wonderful at editing them and making the final copy a joy to read.

Be open with each other and discuss your strengths and weaknesses. Also be sure to discuss your expectations for the book. Here are a few items you should be sure to discuss even before you make an agreement:

(a) Who will do most of the research?

(b) Who do you each see as your target readers?

(c) What do you think the tone will be like — scholarly, more lively, or more general?

(d) How much money do you think it will cost each of you to write this book? Include phone calls, on-line research, travel, and any other extras which could be involved. Estimate high rather than low.

(e) How much money do you think the book will need to earn back for each of you to break even? To make a profit?

(f) What opportunities will each of you forego in order to write this book? What could you be doing otherwise that might be making money? Would those other projects make more or less money?

(g) Who should be in charge? Somebody has to be in charge, even if there are only two of you. Which person will make sure that the manuscript is done and delivered on time?

(h) What should you do if you have a disagreement? (There will be at least a few.) Do you think you can negotiate changes with each other? And don't forget, the editor may change what both of you have wrought.

(i) Who will promote the book? Both of you? One of you? If so, which one of you?

These are only a few of the questions that you should seriously consider before entering into a coauthorship with anyone.

i. HOW TO EVALUATE AN OFFER

It is exhilarating to receive an offer for your work. It's a good idea to step back and evaluate the offer; don't rush to accept.

When you receive an offer, whether it is for a project you've lobbied for or it comes out of the blue, it is important to evaluate it carefully, no matter how big or small.

Here are some things you should consider:

(a) How much research will this project need? How much time will it take me?

(b) How much money is the client offering? Does this include expenses?

(c) How soon is the project due? Do I have time to do it?

(d) Do I know anything about the subject already or am I going to start from zero?

(e) Have I written this type of project before? For example, if the editor wants a personality profile and you've never done one, it doesn't mean that you can't do it — it just means it involves extra learning time.

If you're offered a highly technical job and you feel that it is outside of your knowledge and expertise, don't be dazzled by the money. Turn it down.

(f) Will my work be subject to a lot of review? You need to know this ahead of time. The more people who will look over and critique what you write, the more money you should be paid. A committee of writers is bound to find plenty of changes they think you should make.

Sometimes several of your critics may give opposing advice or directions — this has happened to me! You must find the middle ground.

(g) Who is making the offer? Can your client afford to pay you and does he or she appear to be honorable?

j. MAGAZINES OR BOOKS?

These areas are constantly debated between writers. The crux of the argument (I think) is which pays best. And the answer is really up to you.

Whether writing for magazines, book publishers, or corporate clients, what pays the best depends on the individual, his or her talents, negotiating skills, and ability to get jobs.

Of course, a small newspaper is not going to pay major league dollars and a high circulation magazine is likely to pay well — but there are many other factors to consider. (See chapter 10 for more about negotiating payment.)

That said, it's important to note that book advances generally do not include expenses. They are flat fees, usually with part payable up front and the balance on completion. So the writer who takes on a book project should consider any anticipated expenses before signing a contract.

Magazine fees can range from $50 to a $1,000 or more. If you can churn out magazine copy at a rapid rate, lower-paying markets may not be problematic.

k. TIMING

Timing can work for you. I have obtained some very lucrative assignments over the Christmas holidays and New Year's as well as in the summertime. Why? Because the client needed the job done right away and I was able to meet the deadline.

In a panic, clients seek out writers through networking, computer bulletin boards, and every possible source they can identify.

Before agreeing to such a project, I'd definitely urge you to find out what the "real" deadline is. Often clients give you a deadline that is sooner than when they need to receive it. Why? Because they are used to writers turning in their copy late or they want to leave a comfortable chunk of time for editing.

But when the client is in a big hurry, he or she is much more likely to give you the real deadline. If you can't churn out good copy when the client needs it, turn the job down.

Ask for money up front. People who are in dire straits are more likely to agree to at least some up-front money. Ask for half and settle for about one-third. Remember, you are taking a risk doing a job for a new client and you are also going to be working when other people are out partying. So factor all of that into your price. Remember, you can go out and celebrate when the check arrives.

Realize that editors work well ahead of schedule. Your wonderful article about Christmas should not be submitted in October or November. Think "Christmas in July" and submit it then. Never underestimate the importance of good timing and do your best to take advantage of timing opportunities whenever possible.

l. WRITING FICTION

Although fiction is not my forte, many writers do well writing fiction exclusively or by switching back and forth from fiction to non-fiction. Keep in mind that writing non-fiction involves more than just reporting dull, dry facts. You should also use imagery, descriptions, and fiction-writing techniques in non-fiction as well.

As with non-fiction works, the fiction writer must keep the readers in mind when querying a potential market. You should not submit a novel about a virginal and ethereal young girl to a publisher who is noted for torrid and explicit romances.

So how do you know what they want? Read novels and contact the publishers of the novels you like. Ask for writer's guidelines. Sometimes an author will thank the editor in the acknowledgments to a book. You can direct your query letter to that person. Call the publishing house first to verify that the editor is still there; editors do tend to move around from publisher to publisher quite a bit, particularly in New York City.

If an editor is tentatively interested, novelists are asked to submit more, usually a synopsis of the novel and a description of the characters. The editor may then want to see several chapters or perhaps the entire manuscript.

7

COMMUNICATING WITH EDITORS AND CLIENTS

Often your customers may have little or no experience working with entrepreneurial freelance writers and will not know how to deal with you. You need to educate them and this chapter offers advice on the care and training of your clients.

Sometimes relationships break down and you may no longer get along with an editor or customer. This chapter also covers what to do when that happens.

a. WHAT EDITORS CARE ABOUT

Most editors, like most workers everywhere, want to do a good job, receive praise once in awhile, and, if possible, a promotion. If an editor thinks your well-written pieces can further these goals, then you will be highly valued.

Of course, editors have other goals as well; they want to satisfy their readers. Whether they admit it or not, advertisers are important, too, if the publication is one that accepts ads.

Editors want solidly backed facts and information with quotations that were actually said by the person quoted. They do *not* want to get sued because someone was misquoted. Few writers fake quotes but, unfortunately, some do.

Editors also want copy that captures and holds the reader's attention all the way to the end of the piece.

b. EDITORS ARE PEOPLE

Many new writers forget that editors are human too. They have the power to accept or reject your work, hence they may seem godlike! But they also get stomach-aches, have mortgages, kids, and problems. They have their ups and downs just like everyone else. So how do you deal with editors as professionals but still allow them to be people?

First of all, don't call them just to chat. Be friendly, but be sure each call has a purpose. If you have a hot idea or an important point to make, use the telephone, but keep it brief. If it's not urgent, send a letter, fax, or e-mail message. Be pleasant, but professional.

Also, avoid calling editors on Monday mornings before 10:00 a.m. their time. Always check the telephone directory to see what time zone the editor is in. Many people have the Monday morning blahs, or a staff meeting, or an overstuffed in-basket awaiting them at work. They may not be very responsive.

Avoid calling on Friday afternoon, when people are frantically trying to wrap up their work and don't want any diversions. The day before or after a holiday weekend is another time to avoid, especially in late December.

Always ask the editor if this is a convenient time to call. If not, offer to call back.

Never expect an immediate reply from an editor to your written communications, particularly an editor who is a new client. Some editors may take as long as four to six weeks to reply to a letter. After that time, you may follow up with a polite note or quick phone call.

c. GET IT IN WRITING

Many new and experienced writers rely solely on telephone conversations for the terms and conditions expected by both sides. But memories fail, people become confused, and editors sometimes quit.

Clarify your terms and conditions in writing. Forego, for a moment, your ecstasy about getting the go-ahead and be sure to consider the merits of the actual offer.

If the offer is made to you verbally and the terms and conditions sound reasonable, ask the editor to send you a letter summarizing what you've discussed. Some editors use contracts, while others rely on letters of agreement. Others think a handshake or phone conversation is just fine.

If your editor refuses or never gets around to writing you a contract or letter, one tactic is to "reverse-contract" your client. This means that you summarize the terms and conditions as you understand them and you do it on your letterhead. Still, try to receive some written acknowledgment, such as a note, fax, or letter which states acceptance of your terms.

When the client does send you a contract, read it over carefully. If you don't like the terms and conditions or they seem different from what you thought you had agreed upon, you can either cross out the parts you don't like and initial them or you can request a new contract altogether. If in doubt, or if the contract reads like an insurance policy, ask a lawyer to review it if the fee is for $1,000 or more.

Read the contract! Even major publishers can make silly typographical errors and you don't want some future bureaucrat holding you to a mistaken date or fee.

If the editor verbally promises you something extra that is not in the contract, be sure to get it in writing!

d. DO EDITORS STEAL IDEAS?

New writers often worry unduly about whether magazine, newspaper, or book editors will steal their wonderful ideas. The truth is that it rarely happens.

If you have a great idea, send a query to a publication, and a year later see an article that is *just like* the article you would have written, does it mean that the editor stole your idea?

Probably not. He or she may have already had an article using your idea on file and that's why they turned you down.

Ideas are not copyrightable. If you do feel, however, that your idea is sufficiently unique and that an editor stole your idea, you should register a strong letter of protest with the editor and with the editor's boss, usually the publisher.

It is doubtful that you'll gain any monetary consideration — but it might make you feel better and also make it less likely that the editor will steal any more ideas — if in fact yours was stolen.

e. OTHER CUSTOMERS

Writers deal with many other clients besides editors and publishers. Your clients may span all walks of life and many occupations.

To launch a good working relationship with clients, obtain samples of what they like before you start a project. Ask your prospective client to send you samples of work he or she particularly likes.

If you are writing a business proposal, ask for several winning proposals on which to model yours. If it's a magazine article, ask the editor to send you his or her personal favorite issues of the magazine. If it's a book you are to write, what books did the editor work on and enjoy? Seek out patterns and common denominators.

This doesn't mean you should try to clone what someone else did. If you are hired, presumably the client likes your work. However, what editors and publishers like and what other clients like is different. I write for two editors at the same company and one loves a lot of quotations while the other hates quotes and says they should only be used if absolutely necessary. The different publications they produce clearly show their personal preferences.

f. DEALING WITH CUSTOMERS WHO HAVE NEVER WORKED WITH A FREELANCE WRITER

This happens more frequently than you might imagine, even with editors at established magazines or publishing houses. Editors come and go and may have relied heavily on staff writers. Now, however, many companies have downsized operations and editors have to contract out most of the copy.

Some editors are struggling with the nuances of dealing with a person who isn't on staff; that is, you. Try to make your dealings as pleasant and easy as possible, but do not let the editor (or any other customer) walk all over you.

How might an inexperienced editor take advantage? By constant calls, faxes, last-minute demands, and an unreasonable number of rewrites. You'll recognize it if you see it.

Stand firm. Avoid arguing but stick to the terms of your contract as much as possible. Do one rewrite, not 47. One or two phone calls a day from an editor is pushing it. If he or she calls even more frequently, then there is some insecurity operating here, either with the editor personally, or with you, or both.

If you can tough it out and let the editor's confidence build up, you may want to hang on to him or her, especially if the pay is good. After awhile, if things aren't working out, you should decide whether to drop the client or whether to just grit your teeth and bear it. My personal preference is that dropping a client is much easier on the psyche — and the teeth!

Sometimes customers have no idea how to deal with a contract writer because they never needed to hire a ghostwriter or proposal writer. Help them as much as possible and don't take advantage. Offer a fair price and stand by it.

Virtually all writers are approached at one time or another by people who want someone to write their life story, their marvelous adventure, or something they "just know" will make the *New York Times* bestseller list.

The presumption is that you should be grateful that they're offering you this hot tip. Sometimes they are annoyed when you are not. Be polite and listen (occasionally the person may have a great story idea) but in most cases it is best to tactfully decline such offers because they are usually a waste of your time.

g. WHAT IF YOU DON'T GET ALONG WITH AN EDITOR OR CLIENT?

It happens! One of the beauties of being your own boss is that you can "fire" an editor who you just can't work with.

But before doing that, try to find out what's wrong. First, you can try the direct approach, asking if there's a problem, and if so, what it is. Some people have very controlling personalities and don't mean to patronize or "talk down" to others — it's just the way they are.

You can put up with such behavior or you can argue back when you disagree with the editor. Do remember, however, that he or she is your customer and does have veto power on editorial decisions. Always follow the "business golden rule": he or she who has the gold gets to make the rules.

I once dealt with an editor who seemed to want to argue about everything, no matter how trivial. Argue, argue, argue. Trying to please him was impossible. What worked? Arguing back, telling him he was wrong, and not backing down. He argued less often after I did that. Apparently he appreciated people who fought back. However, there have been editors with whom I could not continue to work. We parted amicably.

Keep in mind though that most editors are normal, reasonable, intelligent beings, just like you.

h. WHAT IF THE EDITOR YOU LIKE QUITS OR IS REASSIGNED?

Frequently, just when you establish a very good rapport with a particular editor — you understand what the editor needs and wants and the editor is very happy with your work — that person leaves and a new editor comes in.

The new editor doesn't know you and perhaps he or she has never worked with a freelance writer before. He or she doesn't return your calls or your letters, even though you are in the middle of a project.

So what can you do? One tactic I have used is to come to a full stop on all work unless and until the editor and I reach some agreement. You can't expect to have the same happy relationship you had with your former editor, but it should at least be a working relationship.

You can send the editor a registered letter saying that you are stopping all work on the project until you can discuss what needs to be done and what direction should be taken.

The probability that you will get an anguished phone call (especially if the editor really needs your project) is quite high. And if you don't hear anything for awhile, don't waste your time working on a project that may ultimately be rejected.

To your surprise, what often happens is that a very good working relationship evolves between you and the new person, one that works so well that when that editor leaves, you will feel sad.

i. WHEN EDITORS AND CLIENTS CALL YOU

After an editor or customer is comfortable working with you, he or she may ask you to do a particular job. The editor tells you how many words are needed, when the deadline is, and so on. All you have to do is say yes or no. Of course, price is also a very serious consideration.

Once an editor trusts you and realizes that you do good work, there's a good chance he or she will call you when something is needed in a hurry. Editors always leave the easy stuff that can be given plenty of lead-time to be done in-house.

When the editor asks if you want to do the job, say, "Well, let me check my schedule. Um, I *think* so." If he or she asks if the amount is enough, never say, "Gosh, I'd do that for free." Be cool. Instead say, "Well, I guess that's fair. But does that include expenses?"

j. MAKING AN EDITOR'S JOB EASIER

Although I have often joked that I don't have to really worry about typographical errors because that's why God made editors, I truly believe it is important to edit your own work very carefully. Even if you have a computer program that can check grammar and spelling, there are still certain things it won't pick up.

When you feel that your draft is pretty much in its final stages, whether it is a report, magazine feature, or an entire book, I recommend you read it very critically *as a reader*, not as an author.

Reread the letter or contract directing you to do the job and make sure you have included what was requested before you send it in. Put a manuscript away for a few days and then come back to it. You'll be amazed at how you will be able to see possible improvements. Read part of the manuscript aloud to hear how it sounds.

Ask yourself these questions:

- Is this interesting and will it keep my reader reading?

- Does it make sense? Are there some statements that are unsupported or not backed up and that should be?

- Is it clear? Are you sure all your readers will understand it?

- If you have used any technical jargon, will it be clear to anyone unfamiliar with the words?

- Do you have a good "flow" and transition of paragraphs from one idea to another? Or are there any sections which seem kind of "stuck" and which take the reader aback?

Read the first paragraph of an article and the last paragraph. Do they seem to have any relationship to each other whatsoever? If the project is lengthy, read the first paragraph of a chapter and the last paragraph. Or you may prefer to read the first and last pages. There should be a common thread that ties together your theme. If not, then make it so.

Read at least part of the piece aloud. When you read aloud, you can often see areas that are problematic that are not obvious when you read silently.

Check for spelling errors and typographical errors and correct them. Perfection is not required but it is a good idea to catch as many errors as you can and get rid of them.

8
RESEARCH BASICS

Research involves finding information from magazines and books, interviewing people, and sometimes searching databases for information. You may need to use several tactics to obtain the needed information.

A key fact or statistic can be the piece of the puzzle that really "makes" your case. Often a quotation from an interviewee is what your reader will walk away remembering. Never underestimate the value of good research.

a. BEFORE YOU START TO RESEARCH: A FEW TIPS

1. Know what you're looking for

Form an outline of your writing assignment either in your head or on paper. After you get focused, determine what you are seeking before you enlist the aid of your librarian and other experts. Don't make busy librarians waste time helping you compile exhaustive research when all you need is general information. (As you learn more, you'll become more adept at picking and choosing your data.)

For instance, do you want to know about the mating pattern of the ibis or are you just looking for more general information? How specific do you need to get? This determines the kind of reference you need.

Your initial outline for your research is important because you need a basic idea of what you're looking for before you go out and actually find it. It's also important to keep in mind that you must be flexible, and if your research reveals that

you're running into a dead end, you can retreat and regroup.

For example, I was recently assigned to research how outpatient providers (primarily doctors and clinics) are reimbursed for their care of nursing home patients. I soon learned that most of the payments are government-controlled. So I decided to investigate a subset of that issue — rehabilitation and physical therapy of nursing-home residents when the nursing home facility directly contracts with a rehab or physical therapy provider.

I would not have known about my final subject if I had not first started out with a basic plan to study nursing homes, gathered names of nursing-home administrators and organizations, and called several people to learn some basics about this subject.

The point I'm trying to get across here is that you should never just walk into a library and ask the frazzled librarian to tell you everything he or she knows about Western civilization or some other topic. Think about what you and your readers would like to know; jot down a basic outline and revise it as you go along.

2. Know your audience

Keep in mind your audience and its reading level. Are your readers academics or are they people who read at the ninth grade level? If you need to keep it simple, you probably don't need to look at highly technical data, exhaustive doctoral dissertations, or academic journal articles.

What questions would your readers be interested in delving into? What are their concerns and biases? As the writer/researcher, you are their representative. Put yourself in their shoes and try to imagine what they care about. People in virtually any field are intrigued by unusual topics, trends, changes in the field, and expert opinions.

3. Who, what, why, where, when, and how

Keep in mind the basics: who, what, why, where, when, and how many. For example, with regard to the ibis, how many are there, anyway? Where are they? Why are they there?

Jot down questions you think readers would ask. You don't have to use them all but they can jog your interest and point to details you might feature.

b. STARTING YOUR RESEARCH

After you make a basic plan, what's next on the agenda? Here are a few suggestions.

1. Make friends with your reference librarian

Most librarians feel a special kinship with writers, so take advantage of this. The reference librarian can be the writer's best friend because he or she can help you find everything ever written on your topic.

You don't have to become your librarian's soul mate. Just be nice to him or her, ask for help, and let him or her know what you're working on. Show some interest in what the library has to offer. It doesn't hurt to donate an occasional bestseller you've already read to your library. Nor does it hurt to acknowledge your librarian, in print, when your first (or subsequent) book comes out.

2. Learn what is available from libraries

Learn what is available in your local library as well as in libraries in neighboring cities. Virtually all libraries have copies of the *Reader's Guide*, a reference publication that lists periodicals that contain articles in different subject areas. In addition, *Books in Print* is another valuable reference for finding books on a myriad of topics or authors both famous and obscure.

Some libraries have their catalogue on a computer database so you can search by subject. I like to browse through the shelves in the subject area I'm researching. Sometimes I've found very useful books that were not listed in the catalogue.

In addition, many libraries today have CD-ROM searchable disks and other services. Some information may also be on microfiche. Ask your librarian.

Libraries have many valuable resources, including vertical files, directories of people and organizations, statistical abstracts, encyclopedias, and much more. It's a good idea for every writer to browse through the library to gain a basic feel of what is available.

Remember that the sources for your research may vary depending on your readers. For example, if you are writing for a Canadian publication, you'll need to consult the *Canadian Periodical Index, Microlog Index, Financial Post Directory of Directors, Who's Who in Canada*, and the *Directory of Canadian Associations*. Once you take on an assignment in a subject area that you are unfamiliar with, you need a reference librarian to point you toward the proper sources.

Don't forget about specialized libraries, such as law, medical, and business libraries in your city or county. Such libraries frequently yield very useful material.

If you are not a member of a particular profession, don't assume you can just walk in and start researching. Instead, call the reference librarian and explain what you want. Ask if it is possible for an outsider to use the library and when. Be sure to say that you are a writer doing research.

This doesn't always work. Once I wanted to look through old files that were no longer in use (i.e., "the morgue") at a newspaper office and I was given an unequivocal "no." But I didn't give up. Instead, I wrote a nice letter to the publisher and he gave me permission.

3. Check bibliographies and appendixes

Once you find magazine articles and books on your topic, be sure to also take a hard look at their bibliographies and appendixes. You may find a reference or source in the appendix that turns out to be more valuable than the book was.

4. Use inter-library loans

Don't forget the inter-library loan service. In many areas, your reference librarian can request documents or books for you through the inter-library loan system. The cost may be free or minimal.

5. Contact clubs, organizations, and trade associations

There are many professional and trade organizations that offer printed information and also help writers identify experts in the field. Check the *Gale Directory* at your library for a vast listing of organizations.

6. Network

Tell your friends, colleagues, and relatives what you're working on. I've obtained great leads from newspaper articles that my mother sent me and ones sent by friends and colleagues. Get the word out.

Don't forget to ask your interviewees if they can recommend anyone you should talk to. Ask for phone numbers. (For more on interviewing, see chapter 9.)

Networking is the ability to ask for what you want without fear or guilt. The worst that can happen is the person will tell you he or she can't help you, and the best is that he or she may provide excellent contacts.

Discreetly name drop during the course of a conversation. This doesn't mean bragging about who you know to impress the person. (Although sometimes it doesn't hurt to try to impress, just a little.) Instead, you can often gain more information by mentioning that Dr. X told you such and such and does your interviewee agree with that or not? This is another valuable tactic for gaining good information.

7. On-line databases

On-line databases can be very valuable, but they often cost money. If I plan to use an on-line database, I arrange to have the client reimburse me for that expense. On CompuServe, I have searched medical and legal databases and many other information gold mines.

I have also received valuable interview contacts on-line. For example, for an article on women accountants, I needed to interview someone from the Midwest. My on-line message netted me a response from someone who knew a female accountant in Ohio.

After screening me through several messages, she gave me the name and number of the accountant. It was a great interview and really made my article.

On another occasion, I read a computer message from a woman who said she was blind and worked for IBM — as a technical writer! Using special equipment, she actually writes software manuals. You can bet my heart beat fast when I read that message. I knew this was a story that I could sell to a magazine for disabled people — and I did.

8. Keep learning

Understand that research is never-ending; there are always more questions to find answers to. In fact, the more you know about something, the more you realize how little you know.

As you learn about your subject, you may find that what you learn does not support your original presumptions or hypotheses. If the overwhelming burden of evidence shows you were dead wrong about something, do not ignore it. First of all, ignoring your mistake is wrong. Second, readers will pillory you in print for ignoring obvious data.

Remember that your project has a due date and will end, whether it is a year from now or a week from now. Many writers get bogged down because they cannot stop researching and start writing.

Just one more fact, just one more interview. They know that there is more information out there and they are right. But the sad truth is that you can never get it all.

Get as much information as you can within the time and budget allowed. The tighter your budget, the more careful you should be about who you call or how far you travel to do your research. Remember, if the project doesn't allow for extra expenses, keep a very close eye on what you spend. Set a limit and don't go over it.

9. Get two sources for one fact

Whenever possible, obtain at least two sources for the same fact. Get some backup documentation, either from a magazine or newsletter article, a report, or another expert. This additional work will enhance what you write.

Be sure to jot down citations of facts that you wish to use. It can be very annoying to read "Experts say..." or "The polls say that..." followed by some startling fact. Be more specific.

Also, try to avoid using polls when possible unless you are illustrating beliefs or opinions. What most people think or believe may be dead wrong.

One of the best ways to obtain timely and unique information is to interview experts in the field. The next chapter discusses important interviewing techniques.

9

EFFECTIVE INTERVIEWING

Research usually involves interviewing people, and every writer needs to become a skilled interviewer. If you don't feel you are adept now, don't worry; this is an attainable skill. Just plan ahead, be adaptable, and listen, listen, listen.

a. MAKING CONTACT

When you call an interviewee or prospective interviewee, often you must reach the person via his or her assistant. He or she may ask who you are "with." Many freelance writers panic, thinking, "I don't really work for the XYZ Corporation, so I can't say I'm working *for* them. But I am doing a job for them. But then...." In the meantime, the assistant waits, increasingly suspicious and impatient.

My policy is that if I'm doing a job for a client, I say, "I'm researching an article for the XYZ Corporation." (Because I am!) Then if the secretary or the interviewee asks how come I'm in Florida and the XYZ Corporation is in Boston, I say that this job has been contracted out to me. Business people understand this because they do it all the time.

I'm not ashamed to say that I'm a freelance writer, but sometimes people's perception of freelance writers as laid-back "cool cats" gets in the way.

The only problem with saying I'm "with" a company is that if I'm working on several different jobs, I have to stop for a moment before I make the phone call and remember who I'm "with" right now!

Speak very confidently as if you deserve to speak to the other person. Speaking this way makes you feel confident, even if you don't start out with that feeling.

Take note of the assistant's name. If she answers, "Ms. Brown's office, Patty Smith speaking," then use the assistant's name. "Hello Ms. Smith, I'm a writer researching an article for XYZ, and I need to speak with Ms. Brown."

If Ms. Brown is too busy and you need to call back later, ask if you can leave a message. When you call back, ask for Pat Smith first and remind him or her that you need to speak to Ms. Brown. The secret behind this gambit is that a person's name is important. Most assistants and secretaries feel very anonymous within a company. After awhile, you may be able to make the assistant your ally in getting Ms. Brown to talk with you.

Often when you call an organization or business, you will be referred to the "public relations" or "media relations" office. Don't worry, this usually doesn't mean that your interview will never happen. In many cases, media relations people can be very helpful in setting up interviews. Tell them who you are and what you need, and they will usually do their best.

b. PRE-INTERVIEW PREPARATION

Many people are afraid to be interviewed. They may have been misquoted in the past or are just generally fearful of the media. It is part of your job to put the person at ease.

Prepare for the interview ahead of time. Here are some basic tips to follow.

1. Set up the interview

Arrange the interview date and time in advance, and tell the interviewee you want to hold it at his or her convenience.

Whether it is an in-person interview or a telephone interview, set up an appointment. Of course, you should be prepared for the possibility that when you call someone to set up an appointment, he or she may say, "Let's do it now!" If the person is otherwise difficult to reach, interviewing him or her on the spot may be wise. However, in most cases interviewees want to set up a time for the interview because it gives them time to think about what they want to say.

2. Set a predetermined place

Set a predetermined place for an in-person interview and make sure your interviewee knows the location. If it is in a building, will you meet in the lobby? If it is in a restaurant, will you meet outside? Make sure this is perfectly clear. It is also a good idea to give the interviewee a brief description of what you look like and your telephone number in case he or she is running late or needs to reschedule.

For a telephone interview, make sure the interviewee knows. It often does not occur to people that interviews can and frequently are conducted by telephone. Consequently, some people will be expecting you to appear in person unless you make it very clear this is a telephone interview.

You can interview the person from his or her office, cellular phone, home, or anywhere else. Some interviewees have called me from the airport or from trade shows.

I strongly recommend against "doing lunch" or meeting at a bar. First of all, the tape recorder picks up all the background noise including other people's conversations, obliterating the one you are trying to conduct.

Second, you will both be preoccupied with eating, not spilling, showing you have good manners, and so on. This wastes time.

I also do not recommend holding the interview in your own home. It is better to meet on neutral turf.

Be sure to tell the interviewee ahead of time how long you think the interview will take, so he or she can schedule enough time. If you need an hour, you don't want to be cut off after 15 minutes.

3. Give the interviewee enough information

Give the interviewee a very basic idea of your topic and your slant but avoid giving all the questions ahead of time. If you give away too much, you're far more likely to get boring and "canned" answers that have been pre-approved by the public relations department.

Sometimes providing the questions up front is the only way to get an interview, so you need to evaluate if this constraint is worth it when it happens.

If you have decided for whatever reason to provide the questions ahead of time, during the interview, ask the questions you've already submitted and slip in a few others that "happen to occur" to you as you talk. In most cases, the interviewee will answer those too, unless your questions are particularly obnoxious or invasive.

4. Prepare your background research

Before the interview, read over any material you have on the subject. Your interviewee will not (or should not) expect you to be an expert but you should try to have a very basic grasp of the topic.

Write down the questions you need to cover and don't want to forget. If one word will jog your memory, use it. Otherwise, write short questions in sentence form. Remember, if the interviewee brings up something that is unique or interesting, it is okay to sacrifice one of your questions to get this new information. The preplanned questions are only a guide.

5. Check your equipment

Does your tape recorder or camera need batteries? Check. Also, if it is an in-person interview, bring an extra tape just in case one tape breaks or the person talks for a longer time than you expected. Before the interview, test the recorder to make sure it works.

For a telephone interview, slide in a tape and take the telephone off the hook before the designated time. Check to see that it records the telephone busy signal or call up and get the weather report and see if it records well.

c. CONDUCTING THE INTERVIEW

If the interview is in-person, you will probably have to spend a few moments accepting or declining coffee, chatting about the weather, and so on. If the interview is by telephone, social niceties can be rapidly dispensed with.

Ask the easy questions first (the ones your interviewee should not mind answering), the hard ones in the middle, and leave the ones you can live without at the end. Why? Because you need those hard questions answered and if you leave them to the end, you may never get to them because of time constraints and other issues.

Even though I recommend taping interviews, I also recommend taking notes during an interview because as the person talks, you may think of a question. Write it down and ask it later.

The tape recorder cannot give you a physical description of the person, so you must jot these details down if they are important. Smoothing away imaginary dust, staring off into space, and other gestures an interviewee may make are details that can reveal character to a reader.

Let's walk through a hypothetical interview to look at its bare bones. Your first interview is at the XYZ Corporation at 9:00 a.m. You arrive five minutes early.

You tell the receptionist you have an appointment to speak with Ms. Wonderful. You decline the offer of coffee or accept it, depending on what you prefer.

Ms. Wonderful comes out, greets you, and leads you back to her office. She offers you a chair and looks at you expectantly. You tell her (again, although you told her before) that you are writing a piece for the *Marvelous* magazine and your basic angle is the female executive in male-dominated fields.

She recalls having talked with you. Now you set up your tape recorder, preferably between you and her so both your voices will come through. If she is seated behind her desk and the distance between you is too great, get closer. Move your chair or ask her to move.

Don't ask permission to use the tape recorder. Unless she is blind, she can see what it is. Over the telephone, the interviewee cannot see the recorder. You don't ask permission then either, but you do announce that you are taping the interview.

If there are any pauses in conversation or your interviewee is called away for a few moments, rewind the tape a little bit and make sure it is recording. (I have been known to bring two recorders to an interview, but that is usually not necessary.)

d. CATEGORIZING INTERVIEWS

Interviews are either easy or hard. For a novice, all interviews may be hard. They should never all be easy, or you're doing something wrong — there needs to be an edge to at least some of your interviews. It helps to keep you on your toes.

1. Easy interviews

Many interviews are a pleasure. This is particularly true if you are profiling someone who wants to be written about or when you are interviewing an expert who loves his or her field.

Sometimes you need only listen and guide the interviewee every once in awhile if he or she strays off the topic. Other times you will need to ask many questions, but these may be ones that are obvious and it will be easy to get answers.

However, you can never assume that every interview will be easy or that you can turn off your listening ears.

2. Hard interviews

An interview can be difficult because you feel uncomfortable with the subject or have some other problem. This is something you can work on. Familiarize yourself with the topic and then quit worrying.

More frequently, interviews can be difficult because the interviewed person is uncomfortable or upset. No matter how effective an interviewer you are and how wonderful you are as a person, there will inevitably be times when people do not want to talk with you. However, you need to do the interview. One tactic is to try to find out why the person doesn't want to talk with you. It may be a bad time, or he or she doesn't feel well, or is facing a personal crisis. You may never find out the reason.

If you call a person and aren't greeted warmly, don't take it personally. Tell the person you will call at another time when it is more convenient. Most people respond to politeness.

Another reason is paranoia. The person is afraid to talk to journalists because he or she fears being misquoted and risking his or her position. Maybe this person *has* been misquoted in the past and has suffered.

When I encounter this fear (and you can usually tell when people are afraid of being interviewed by their behavior, tone of voice, and lack of eye contact), I tell people that I am not "60 Minutes" and I am not seeking out their innermost personal thoughts or fears. (This is true, by the way.)

Often, just getting the fear out in the open is a great disarmer. I also tell the person that I tape record all interviews because I want to make sure I get the quotes right. In addition, I tell the person that the only changes I would make would be if the person made a misstatement and said "are" instead of "is" or made some other small grammatical error.

e. EFFECTIVE LISTENING

Two people could interview the same person at the same time and hear exactly the same words. The better listener gains the most.

Many people think they are effective at listening, but studies have revealed that much of what is said never reaches our brains. We start out intending to be good listeners; we watch the person's body language, listen to the tone of voice, and try to follow the words. Then our concentration slips and we start thinking other thoughts. Resist them!

Concentrate on what the person is saying. This doesn't mean you fix your eyes on him or her; that can be quite unnerving. In an in-person interview, just listen and glance away periodically.

Sometimes you may hear noises outside or the room may be too hot or too cold. If you can control these things, do so. Ask if you can shut the window. Put on your jacket if you're cold or take it off if you're hot. If you don't have control, ignore these things.

Your interviewee may distract you. Someone's appearance and body language can shift your attention from what he or she is saying to what he or she is wearing or doing.

Identify ahead of time your own personal distracters, whether it is a person's dress, accent, or words and phrases that annoy you. For example, I loathe the phrase, "He's dead meat!"

The problem is that when we are bothered, we lose focus and become inattentive. Yet your interview subject with the annoying verbal tic also has valuable information.

Try to focus beyond the oft-repeated "you know?" and concentrate on the underlying points. What has he or she said about the subject? Are profits up or down? Are more widgets being made, or fewer?

Try to paraphrase what you think the subject has said to you. "Mr. Jones, it sounds as if within the next two years, your company may well be number one in your field." If you're wrong, he'll tell you. If you're off-course, he'll tell you. And if you're dead-on, he'll tell you.

Do not be afraid to be wrong or confused about something. It is better to ask a question now that you may consider "stupid" rather than to write something wrong and annoy your editor and readers later on.

Are there trends and changes in the interviewee's field? Do not worry about memorizing quantities. You should be taping anyway. Instead, look for things like percentage improvements or worsening or flattening out if you are interviewing a business person.

f. REFLECTIONS ON INTERVIEWING AND INTERVIEWEES

Based on my experience of interviewing people for well over a decade, it seems to me that depending on someone's occupation, he or she will be either easy to interview or difficult. Your experience may prove different from mine but let me share what I have learned to date.

So far, police officers have proven to be the most difficult to interview. They are the most challenging subjects to extract information from. This may be due to their job. People probably lie to police officers a lot.

I have spent inordinate amounts of time working to convince a police officer that I would not misquote him or her and that I would use the information to a good end.

So how do you interview a cop? Make arrangements well ahead of time, tell him or her exactly what you want to do, why, and show up on time for the interview.

Conversely, I have found lawyers to be very easy to interview. I wondered if it is because lawyers think they could sue me if they don't like what I say, but I don't really think that's it. Lawyers are very verbal people and are used to communicating information. They are also very analytical.

As you might guess, politicians are generally easy to interview, as long as you don't need to nail them down on specifics. If you use them to discuss their views in general, they are wonderful interviewees. Politicians are easy to obtain access to. They want press! Of course, if you're talking about a president or prime minister, that's far more difficult to arrange.

Call the press secretary and explain why you want to interview the politician and who you are writing the piece for. If it is a magazine, you will probably be asked what its circulation is, so find out ahead of time.

Physicians are fairly easy to interview, but the hard part is getting to them. They are constantly darting about from place to place and it is hard to find a time when you can actually talk to one. Telephone interviews are best when you want to interview a doctor.

College and university professors are not difficult to interview but they seem to love to expound on theory and you must keep them on track to get practical details. If you do an in-person interview, you may find the professor lecturing at you as if you were a student. Let him or her go on if you are getting useful data. If not, interrupt with your questions.

Sometimes highly educated people who are affluent are more worried about their status and how what they say might possibly affect them. They may worry about getting fired or not getting promoted if they're rising stars in the corporation. Expect them to refer you to the public relations department and sometimes to try to duck an interview altogether.

Try to disarm such a person with honesty and charm; some you'll never win over, and you must accept this.

Tradespeople and nonprofessionals are often initially a little nervous about being interviewed but far less timorous than those who have, or think they have, a lot to lose.

I cannot generalize by gender. Some men are tough to interview and some women are easy and vice versa. Women often speak too softly and your tape recorder may not pick up everything. You can either ask softspoken people to speak up or speak very low yourself, so that they ask you to speak up. This makes them speak up.

I think people over age 40 are generally easier to interview, but that may be in part because I am over age 40. Retired people are frequently eager to be interviewed, possibly because they have more time and also because they want to share their experiences with others.

In my experience, children under the age of 12 are too squirmy and easily distracted to be good interviewees. On the other hand, adolescents are too worried about their appearance and how their peers will react to what they say.

Sometimes people from other countries can be difficult to interview because they don't know the right words to convey their thoughts or they're afraid that they don't know them. They may underestimate their own abilities. Avoid using "slanguage" when speaking with someone from another country. If he or she uses a term you are not familiar with, ask politely for an explanation.

g. INTERVIEWING TIPS

1. Check spelling

Ask the person to spell his or her first and last name. Sometimes "John Smith" is really "Jon Smyth." Even the most ordinary-sounding names may have a special spelling. Also make sure you get his or her full and proper title at work, if that is important.

2. Be neutral

Don't let your own opinions or views intrude too much. The purpose of an interview is to get information and good quotes; it's not just a conversation.

If you have strong views about a subject, be careful about sharing them. Your interviewee may not share your views and it could damage your ability to get information from him or her.

There are also some subjects that it is best to avoid. Abortion, for example, is a subject that people have strong feelings about. A good writer has to remain objective.

3. Let your interviewee dominate the interview

Let your interviewee dominate the interview, but don't be afraid to interrupt if he or she is stuck in the talk-only mode. You need information and you have a limited time in which to gather it.

So if your interviewee keeps rushing off on a tangent, don't stay silent. Most people stop to take a breath once in awhile, so when that happens, ask your next question.

Another way to get people to stop talking is to keep silent — that is, don't say, "Really?", "Oh?", or any of those other encouraging words. Say nothing. Most people become uncomfortable and stop talking.

4. Get the interviewee talking

What if the interviewee won't start talking? You could tell the interviewee you are not an investigative reporter and you want some good basic information, not innermost secrets or thoughts. Of course, don't say this if it's not true.

Another tactic with a person you sense is negative is to say, "I guess you're a person of few words." I used this in a desperate attempt to get a particularly stubborn person to talk. It worked. To disprove what I had said, he spoke at great length.

5. Create interview questions that work

Think of questions that will elicit thoughtful responses, not yes or no answers. Do not phrase the question in a negative way. "You don't think the economy is going to change, do you?" implies that he or she is not supposed to think it's going to change.

Don't ask the question in a positive way either. "You do think the economy is going to get better, right?" Don't give away the "right" answer in your question. Presumably, your interviewee is the expert and you are not.

Try for a neutral approach. "What do you think will happen with the economy over the next six months?" is one possibility. Or "Where do you see the economy headed?" is acceptable, but your interviewee may then ask what time frame you're talking about. Then you could amend your question and ask about where he or she thinks the economy is headed over the next six months.

Be sure to avoid too many questions that can earn you a meager yes or no. You can't use those responses for quotations. If you do receive a yes or no response, however, press on and ask why, when, and how much.

h. LISTENING SKILLS FOR THE IN-PERSON INTERVIEW

Eye contact is important, but don't stare! Ask your question and then shut up. Your only response, during breaks, should be affirmative comments such as "Yes, I see."

If the person talks too long, stop making affirming comments. If necessary, cough or gaze distractedly away. Most people catch on. Try to avoid interrupting unless you must. When your interviewee pauses, try to summarize what has been said: "It sounds like you are saying that..." and listen to see if you got it right.

Don't worry about memorizing statistics; this is why you brought your tape recorder. Instead, try to determine what the statistics or figures mean: are things better or worse? Always ask for an explanation. Don't be afraid of seeming stupid because you don't understand something. Get the interviewee to explain any jargon or special terms; your readers will want to know too.

Don't be a slave to your list of questions. Sometimes an interviewee makes a startling or unusual remark that could lead to some very good information. Follow up.

If an interviewee evades your question, ask it again later, reworded.

Notice where the interviewee sits. Does the interviewee hide behind a big desk, sit next to you, or stand and look down upon you? These are all clues to the person.

At some point in the interview, say something positive. Unless you're interviewing a mass murderer, you should be able to find something to say that is positive and you believe is true. Never make insincere small talk.

Sadly, most people are starved for positive feedback. The slightest favorable comment can often elicit a great deal of information.

i. LISTENING SKILLS FOR THE TELEPHONE INTERVIEW

Make an appointment for the telephone interview, just as you would for an in-person interview. Tell the person you have recorded this date on your calendar and ask him or her to record it as well. Give your telephone number.

Be polite and friendly but keep any small talk to a minimum.

Listen for changes in voice; be sensitive to changes in pitch. If the person starts to fade out, you can try speaking very softly, which tends to make people speak up, or you can start talking more loudly. You can also try asking the interviewee to speak up.

If the person rambles on and on, be completely silent. Most people will stop talking. Silence also works after you ask a question. Ask it and shut up and listen.

Don't be afraid if your interviewee is silent for a few moments; he or she may be framing an answer. Give the interviewee a chance to answer.

Sometimes you must interrupt because you need to get your interviewee back on track. Always be polite; an interview is an exchange between two professionals, not a social occasion.

j. SOLUTIONS TO COMMON INTERVIEW PROBLEMS

Problem #1: The assistant protects the boss from all evil invaders, especially those who telephone.

Solution: Be self-confident but not arrogant. Explain what you're trying to do: for example, researching an article on ABC for XYZ. Explain how much time you need. In most cases, you won't need more than an hour.

Then politely ask when would be a good time to call. If the assistant says "never" (most would never say that, but there are some diehards), offer alternative times.

Late afternoon? Right after work starts? Lunchtime? Get the assistant's name.

Then, the next time you call, ask for the assistant or secretary by name. State that you are the person who called yesterday and wondered if Mr. Wonderful might be available this week to talk with you. Always be polite and friendly. It usually works!

Problem #2: The interviewee asks to see the article or the manuscript before submission or wants to approve any quotes. However, your editor says never, ever show your copy to anybody else.

Solution: Tell your interviewee that you will tape the interview (and I think you should) and that you are very careful when it comes to accuracy. You can explain that many writers, including reporters from major newspapers, do not tape and this is probably one reason why people may sometimes get misquoted.

I also assure my interviewees that the only changes I make to quotes are minor rewordings to correct grammar. This is very appreciated and relieves most people.

Problem #3: You've asked a question and the interviewee has not answered. Instead he or she has responded by talking about something else. This is very common among politicians and people who have media savvy.

Solution: Ask several other questions, then reframe your original and unanswered question, using different words. Try up to three times. If this doesn't work, you're probably not going to get the answer.

Problem #4: You need some information and the interviewee has said that he or she is not going to give it to you. For example, you need to know about how much the company grossed last year, and the interviewee says that is confidential information.

Solution: You probably have at least a vague feel of how much the company makes. Let's say you think it's around $20 million. Say to the reluctant interviewee, "I understand, but we need a rough ballpark figure for our readers. So I'm guessing you're at around $10 million."

In most cases, the interviewee will forget all about confidentiality and say, "What?! Ten million! We grossed $21.47 million last year and this year we're going to top $23 million!" At this point, you are very impressed and apologize for accidentally slighting the company. Now that you have it right, you won't make that mistake.

See Samples #8, #9, #10 on the following pages. These samples provide questions as guides for what you can ask in your interviews. Adapt them according to your own needs and topics.

If you would like more information on developing interview skills, you may want to refer to *How to Interview*, another title in the Self-Counsel Series.

1. What is the hardest part about this job (or industry, field, etc.)? Why do you consider it the hardest part?

2. What is the biggest mistake people in this field make?

3. Where do you see this field (or your career) headed over the next three to five years? Why?

4. What do you like best about this field? Why?

5. What is a typical day like for you?

6. What are the trends in this field? Why?

7. Are there any other experts in this field who you would recommend? Do you have their telephone numbers?

8. There is no way you could tell me everything you know about this subject. But is there anything we haven't discussed that you think is important for readers to know? (Define who your readers are: Human resources executives, teachers, etc.)

9. Who else in this field do you recommend that I contact?

1. Where were you born and raised?

2. When you were growing up, did you ever imagine that some day
   you'd become a _____? (e.g., successful executive, famous ballerina, etc.)

3. What is a typical day like for you?

4. What personality trait makes you successful?

5. What is the hardest part of your job?

6. What would you change about your career field if you had magical powers?

7. What is the most fulfilling aspect of your career?

8. Where do you hope to be, five years from now?

9. What are your hobbies?

10. Who is your favorite author?

11. Who do you admire most?

12. Did you have a mentor in your career? Who was it and what did he or she do?

SAMPLE #10
THE HOW-TO INTERVIEW

1. How long did it take you to learn how to...? (e.g., build log cabins, grow rare orchids, etc.)

2. How long would it take the average person?

3. What is the best part about learning how to do this?

4. What is the hardest part?

5. Describe the process for me, from start to finish.

6. What materials do you need?

7. Does a person need any special training or equipment to achieve this goal? (Whatever it is.)

8. What is the biggest mistake people doing this make? Any others?

10
MONEY AND GETTING PAID

The "bottom line" — money left over after you pay your expenses and taxes — is important to all businesses. Therefore, it is important to address the mind-set issue again.

When you're working for a corporation or the government, you expect to receive your weekly or biweekly paycheck. You may be worried about stretching it to meet your bills, but you do know it's coming. Not true when you are a business owner.

In your own writing business you're owed money for jobs, but it's your responsibility to make sure you price a job right and that you get paid.

Before we get into pricing, I'd like to say that a job that pays $200 may be a better deal for you than a job that pays $1,000. Why? Because the job that pays $1,000 may include no expenses and require many hours of work, whereas the job that pays the "mere" $200 may be a simple task for you. This is important! You must take into consideration how many hours a job will take and how hard it is.

a. HOW TO PRICE A JOB

Although you may feel comfortable knowing how much is fair for a magazine piece or a book contract, very often you'll be asked to do a job you've never done before and you must decide how much to charge. So how do you decide?

1. Ask your colleagues

Ask your colleagues what they have charged for similar jobs, especially if they are not in the same geographic location as you and are not competitors. Find out if they generally ask for one flat rate and if they receive reimbursement for expenses. Do they ask for money up front? Do they ask for periodic progress payments?

2. Determine your own profit margin

Despite what your colleagues may receive, you should also determine if this job will be profitable for you. Set an hourly rate that you'd like to earn and don't make it too low. Writers are more likely to underbid than overbid.

For example, let's say you'd like to earn $40 per hour. Remember, you have overhead expenses to cover and $40 payable to you as an entrepreneur is not the same as $40 payable to you as an employee, where your employer picks up the overhead and pays employee benefits.

Now, determine how many hours you think this job will take. Break the job up into segments. If it is a special report, ask for samples of previous special reports, so you can see what the job is supposed to look like at completion.

Does the client want you to first submit an outline or a rough draft of the project? Or does he or she not want to hear from you until you are close to completion?

Determine how many parts there are to this project and what kind of work will go into it. Perhaps the job will require ten hours of research and 20 hours of writing, for a total of 30 hours.

This is *not* the figure you give the client; we're not finished yet! Next, find out if this job includes or does not include expenses, such as on-line research and telephone and fax expenses. If it does not, then you should add enough hours to compensate for that lack.

Even if the client will pay an add-on for expenses, you should take a very hard look at the number of hours you've come up with. Why? Because things take longer than we expect them to. Add in a "fudge factor" of at least 25% or more depending on how good you are at pricing jobs. Add 25% at least for a new client and a new kind of job.

Should you bill the client at an hourly rate? I avoid it whenever possible because there is a tendency for the client to presume or suspect you may be dragging your feet if you're paid by the hour. But if you're being paid by the job, it's in your own best interests to do the job well and promptly.

3. The aggravation factor

Don't forget to consider the aggravation factor, a term I use to describe how difficult you think a project will be. If this is a client you've worked with before and you know he or she is difficult, then you'll have a higher aggravation factor. If this is a new client, there is an aggravation factor because you don't yet know if you'll be able to work well together. For a new client I add in an aggravation factor of at least 10%.

If I've worked with someone before and we got along well, that client gets a zero aggravation factor. A former client who has given me grief — yet pays enough to compensate — could get any range of aggravation factors.

What else is aggravating? For me, it is being given a week to do a difficult job. Clients who constantly change their minds are aggravating.

You can use the aggravation factor as part of your pricing strategy. Also, if someone offers you a certain amount of money for a job, you can use the aggravation factor to determine if it is going to be worth it.

Figure out what you need to earn times the number of hours you think the job will take. Always overestimate the number of hours. Too many writers tend to think a job will be easier than it turns out to be. Consider whether your telephone, fax, and travel expenses will be paid by the client. Then, when that total is determined, add on the aggravation factor to obtain your final price.

4. The "fun" factor

Another consideration is whether the project appeals to you. You might consider taking on a lower-paying assignment because it has an element of fun. You adore working with the editor, so any assignment with him or her is a plus. Your fun factor could be 10% or more, depending on the project.

Some people may think factoring in fun is silly, but I feel that enjoyability should be taken into account, at least sometimes.

A fun factor is *deducted* from the price you've calculated because you're willing to take less in order to work on this project. Assign a fun factor to special projects only.

A job is fun if I know and like the editor and the subject sounds fascinating. If I am given enough time to do the job at an unhurried pace, that is fun too.

It is important to note, however, that in some, if not many cases, you will still need to turn down projects that are fun. You are in business to make money and not to be entertained.

5. Other sources of information

There are other sources to check for types of fees charged. For example, the *Writer's Market*, published annually, provides general information on how much writers charge for many types of jobs. In addition, it gives ranges of fees paid to writers by various publishers.

Remember, these figures are not cast in stone! A client may offer you less, but often will offer you more if you appear to be worth it.

6. Fees for complicated jobs

If the job requires you to interview many people, take that time into account when you calculate the time needed to do the job. If you transcribe your tapes, take that time into account as well.

If your project is subject to review by more than two or three people, be sure to add plenty of extra hours. The more people there are involved in a project, the more difficult it is.

What about the job turnaround? If the client needs the job very quickly, say in a week or a month, he or she may be willing to pay more than usual out of desperation.

Why not charge more, since you will have to work harder? If you were working overtime in a supermarket, you'd expect to get paid extra. So why should it be different if you're a writer?

Another factor to consider is how much the client can afford; this can be tough. If the client is business-savvy, he or she will not want to tell you what the limit is; you should ask anyway. "What's your projected budget for this assignment?" is a polite way to find out how much you will be offered.

Try hard to delay the discussion of money. The one who brings up a figure first loses. Your client may have deep pockets and can make you a very generous offer. After all, you're worth it! On the other hand, he or she is not going to spend extra money if it can be avoided.

So what you should do is show your fascination and interest in the project. Ask a lot of questions, describe similar work that you have done, mention contacts who can assist you, and get your client interested in giving you the job.

Another factor to consider is your own level of expertise. If you have written on the topic many times before, then your background and knowledge lends extra value to the project. Also, if you have contacts in the field on whom you can rely, these also add value.

Should you add on 10% or 20%? Only you can determine how much extra to add on because of your experience level and other unquantifiable factors. Samples #11, #12, and #13 at the end of this chapter show how to price different projects and decide whether to accept or reject them.

b. WHEN TO ASK FOR MONEY UP FRONT

When you're offered a lengthy job that will take weeks, or months, or longer, or one that pays $2,000 or more, you should always ask for money up front. This is particularly important when you are beginning your writing business. Many writers have worked hard on projects for which they were never paid.

The client wasn't necessarily dishonest. Disasters can happen; clients become ill, companies go out of business, etc. For your protection and security, ask for money up front whenever possible. Call it a retainer, or an advance, or whatever name you feel comfortable with.

How much should you ask for? I'd ask for at least one-third of the total job up front, or half if you think you can get it. Beyond that, it's doubtful if the client would agree.

Actually, this up-front money has a good psychological advantage for both you and your client. You have some money in your pocket and you're motivated to do the job. He or she has paid you and can expect you to produce results — and has the right to contact you periodically to find out how you're doing.

c. EXPENSES

Expenses can be billed on a monthly basis or at the end of the job, whichever is more convenient. When your client is new, he or she may request copies of telephone bills and other receipts as well as an annotated list with your invoice.

What expenses do most clients accept? Telephone and fax charges and overnight mail service fees are usually acceptable expenses. Travel expenses can be included too, if this was agreed upon beforehand.

Some expenses are presumed to be part of your overhead. For example, few clients cover the cost of your diskettes, paper, or postage. Some clients will return diskettes to you for your reuse, but that's not common.

Make sure that you both agree on what kind of expenses are to be covered, no matter who your client is.

Sometimes your client will request an upper limit on expenses; for example, you may bill for up to $200 in telephone expenses and after that you have to pay them. Clients put a cap on expense claims to discourage freelancers from taking advantage of their largesse. As a writer and researcher, you need to make the most efficient use possible of your telephone.

However, if your client suddenly needs you to call someone in Geneva, Switzerland (and this has happened to me!), then you should be able to add on such special expenses.

d. CONTRACTS

The word "contract" really scares a lot of people. Contracts can be full of confusing legal jargon that only lawyers can understand, but they don't have to be.

A contract is an agreement between at least two people and it can be oral or written. In the writing business, it should be written.

Many of your clients have their own standard contract forms that they will ask you to sign. Read them over and sign them if they seem fair. If there's something in a contract that you don't like, cross it out and initial it.

It could be a minor clause that everyone ignores anyway, but it might be something that could cost you the job! But remember, you are in this to make a profit and you should not take on jobs that will cost you money with no other benefit in sight.

When you first contact a possible client, often by letter, he or she may telephone you and tell you to go ahead since your terms are fair. Always ask if the client can send you a note to that effect on company letterhead.

If he or she cannot or will not, then you should send a written letter summarizing your understanding of what the client wants you to do, how much you'll receive, and when to send it. This is called "reverse contracting." This tactic has always worked well for me.

A written contract is important because it spells out what is expected of everyone. If there is any disagreement later on, you have the contract to refer to. With no contract, your client could say he or she wanted 20,000 words, not 2,000! If there is no written agreement about extra expenses, then the client could say that the fee includes all expenses. The contract should spell out any up-front money to be paid as well as the total fee.

The time frame should also be included. If the work is to be completed in sections, list the dates on which each part has to be done. For example, you may need to submit the first draft on April 15th and the final on June 30th. Although it isn't required, I usually offer one free rewrite.

The contract should also describe what materials the client may provide, like leads, contacts, data, records, etc.

Sometimes you need to include protection clauses that both parties agree to beforehand, to avoid misunderstandings in the future.

It's not that people are out to rip you off — the problem is that people often forget the details of agreements they've made over the telephone or in person. You probably forget occasionally too.

Most of the contracts I sign for jobs under $2,000 are one-page documents written by the client or one- or two-page letter agreements written by me.

e. INVOICES

I am baffled by the attitude among many writers that invoices are somehow tacky or even unprofessional. You've agreed to do a job and when it is done, you should bill the client, whether he or she is an editor, a corporate vice president, a ghostwriting client, or anybody else. Book publishing contracts usually give authors royalties on each copy sold, so you won't know how much you have earned until you receive your royalty statement. A check to cover royalties usually comes with the statement.

Many writers advise billing the accounting department directly and skipping the editor's in-basket whenever possible.

Many clients expect invoices and will give you a purchase order number to place on your invoice. This is good, because that means that accounting has already budgeted for your work and is planning to pay you. Sometimes you will receive two purchase order numbers: one for the main job and one for expenses.

Invoice forms are readily available in office supply stores and you can also buy them by mail order. However, I recommend you buy an inexpensive computer invoice program because the invoice printouts look more professional and also provide you with a good way to track your payments. Many invoice programs allow you to look at a register of all your receivables. (Money owed to you is receivable. Money you owe is accounts payable.) Sample #14 at the end of this chapter shows an invoice.

Remember, when you invoice customers, most clients won't pay you for about 30 days because that is an industry standard. If you've negotiated to receive immediate payment, be sure to state this on the invoice itself. You still may not get paid for 30 days!

In many cases, you won't have much — if any — negotiating room on what you will be paid. But if you are venturing into work for businesses or ghostwriting work, and sometimes in the case of magazine writing, you may be asked how much you charge.

f. WHAT IF YOU DON'T GET PAID?

Sometimes that awful thing happens — money that is owed to you is not paid. The editor doesn't return your calls, the article has been published, and you're worried you're never going to see that check. You had a contract, you invoiced them, but still, no payment. Should you give up?

No! Editors are sometimes great with words and awful with money. They may forget to turn in your invoice to the accounting department, lose it, or just consider it a low priority.

You can also call. If the editor won't speak to you, will the publisher? Contacting the publisher directly has worked for me.

You can write dunning letters too, but I advise holding off on those. Everyone hates threats and that's your final piece of ammunition in the battle, so you don't want to use it right away.

Sometimes writers' groups will intercede for you and they have varying track records at recovery. Also, in some cases, writers' groups have contracted with actual collection agencies.

The fee should be over several hundred dollars or a collection agency is not interested. (They keep a percentage of the amount collected.)

It is also important to note that when a client owes you money that was due over 60 days ago, you should not do any more work for that client. This seems self-evident, yet many writers continue to write, essentially for free. This is not good practice.

Holding off on providing any further copy may be just the incentive the company needs to release your money to you.

Are there times when you just won't get paid or shouldn't pursue payment? Yes, for example, when a client still owes you $25 and it would cost you three hours to collect it in letters, phone calls, and so forth — and you still might not collect — it may not be worth pursuing. Sometimes it's worth it to write it off as a bad debt.

I think many writers give up far too easily, but there is a point where it is unreasonable to keep going. You will need to determine where that point is for you.

SAMPLE #11
PRICING A NEW CLIENT

Hourly rate you need	$50
Hours you think job will take	20 hours (*Estimate high)
Expenses? Will publisher pay?	No
If no, anticipated expenses	$500
Total	$1,500
Aggravation factor	10%
You need to receive	$1,650

*In estimating how many hours a job will take, include phone calls, trips to the library, typing, and just plain thinking.

SAMPLE #12
DECIDING TO TURN DOWN A JOB

Client offers you	$800
Hourly rate you need	$40
Hours job will take	30
Client pays expenses?	Yes
Total	$1,200

Aggravation/Fun factor (This is a tough client!)   20%

You need	$1,440

Turn this job down unless you can negotiate for more.

SAMPLE #13
DECIDING TO ACCEPT A JOB

Client offers you	$500
You need	$30 per hour
Job will take	20 hours
Aggravation factor	0 (You love this client)
Total	$600
Fun factor	20% (i.e., you deduct 20% from price to do this fun job)
Total	$480

Go ahead and do the job.

Wally Writer
4 Treehouse Court
Columbia, ME 00000

INVOICE 462
DATE 7/25/9-

XYZ Corporation
59 Elm Street
Columbia, ME 00000

30 days
_____

Description	Amount
Article of tree pruning for October issue	400.00
Expenses (see attached annotated list)	57.00
Subtotal	457.00
Total	$457.00
Amount paid	$0
Amount due	$457.00

11
RECORD KEEPING

Although you may not enjoy it, as a business person you need to keep and maintain orderly records.

Keep track of your expenses, including telephone, stationery, printing, and photocopies as well as large expenditures for equipment. You'll need this information for tax deductions, depreciation expenses, and to figure out if you are making a profit.

a. TELEPHONE AND FAX EXPENSES

Although some writers scoff at tracking telephone calls, I think it is very important for writers to note all long distance calls, including who was called or faxed, when, and the telephone or fax number. When you get your telephone bill, write in how much each call cost.

There are several advantages to tracking calls. First, as mentioned in past chapters, if you are being reimbursed for your telephone expenses, then you can verify that you made the calls.

Often you may need to call former interviewees back, either to clarify something they said or to use them for a new piece you are writing. So if you can look up the telephone number in your log, you save valuable time.

In addition, once you get used to tracking your calls, you will consciously and unconsciously develop a grasp of the reasonable amount of time for a telephone call, depending on the subject, who your client is, and how much he or she pays.

As a result, you are more practical and more efficient; you may realize that it might be good for you to call some interviewees after 5:00 p.m., especially if you are on the east coast and they are on the west coast, in order to take advantage of lower rates.

Even when the client covers your expenses, when you run up expensive telephone bills, it is you who has to front the costs. When you get your bill, submit an invoice. Thirty days later you may be paid. You lose the use of that money for over a month, affecting your cash flow. Also, your client doesn't pay you any interest, just the exact amount charged. Consequently, it is cost-effective for you to be frugal whenever possible, even when expenses are reimbursable. Keeping track of telephone bills helps you trim expenses.

Some writers believe it is all right to offer an estimate of expenses and not bother to keep track. The problem is that you end up undercharging your customer.

It is true that recording and later tracking telephone calls takes time. However, it takes only a few minutes to record your calls for the day. You can jot them down after each call or at the end of the day. This is much easier than trying to reconstruct your record of calls a month later when the bill arrives.

Another advantage of recording your calls is that experts, consultants, and other interviewees are excellent sources for future articles, books, or projects. So if you have recorded your calls in a phone log or some other format, you can just look up the name and telephone number and contact that person.

You can also maintain a Rolodex (electronic or manual) of important contacts. You never know when you might need to contact that person again.

Include the name of the client with your telephone log. This is useful if you are working for several clients at the same time. I generally write down the first name of the editor and that works for me. You may want to write down first and last names and/or the name of the publication.

I also recommend that telephone logs be set in one stand-alone book or notebook (see Sample #15).

b. RECORD YOUR EARNINGS

Record the checks you receive as they start coming in. Many people keep a record of revenues in the same place they record expenses. If you have an invoice program, you can input the payment when it is received.

Record when the check was received, who it was from, the amount, and the name of the publication or company.

Try to record payments (and expenses) the day it happens. You think you'll never ever forget a check for $2,000 or more and you may not. However, later you may ask, when did it come? Was it June or July? Was in 1993 or 1994? Keep a record and you'll know for sure.

c. OTHER EXPENSES

An entrepreneurial writer incurs many overhead expenses that clients cannot cover: paper, postage, diskettes, and other items. Maintain a listing of these expenses for your own purposes (as well as for tax purposes) so you know how profitable you are and what areas you need to improve on.

For example, if you find your paper expenses seem very high, is it because you print out every single draft that you've written? Wouldn't it be more cost-effective

and efficient, in such a case, to compose directly on the computer and print out only a final draft, if that?

The more aware you are of your spending patterns, the better you can control them. Businesses are always looking for ways to cut expenses, and you, as a businessperson, should also make attempts to improve your bottom line through cutting costs.

d. TAXES

Although taxation is certainly a topic that makes most people groan, it is important to keep in mind that a profit-making writer will need to pay income tax.

It is impossible to cover all or even a small part of the tax issues involved in running a home business. The point is that without adequate records, you will be unable to assess what taxes you owe and nobody else will be able to either. You certainly do not want to overpay.

In some cases, your clients can provide you with that information. In the United States, most clients send writers annual statements that show how much was paid in the previous year. These forms are also sent to the Internal Revenue Service. Always check with your government tax office for the latest requirements.

In Canada, contact Revenue Canada for more information on the records you need to keep and the deductions you are eligible for. You will also need to decide if you are going to charge GST. (For more information, see *The GST Handbook*, another title in the Self-Counsel Series.)

e. A PERSONAL JOURNAL

I use a personal journal as a place to record my goals and achievements as well as what I hope to accomplish over the next few months. It is informal and written in longhand, so probably no one but me could read it, but I consider it another record keeping device and one that helps me keep on track and be more organized. A journal can also be a very good place to write down ideas and generate creativity.

f. PROJECT RESEARCH AND RECORDS

Although not required by tax authorities or your clients, I think it is a good idea to retain the research material for a project for at least a year or so. You can go back and use it again if you need to or you can answer any questions that may come up after your work is published.

Choose an appropriate file folder for the size of the project and label it. For voluminous projects, you may want to use heavy accordion-style folders or even boxes. For smaller projects, use file folders.

When you come up with a way to spin off an old idea, you can pull out that folder and reuse and update the material.

g. BUSINESS CORRESPONDENCE

It is also important to maintain at least several correspondence files. If you're a heavy communicator, you may want to make monthly or semi-annual folders. If you don't write or receive a lot of letters, then you could make an annual file.

I recommend you create a file for "Letters Received" and a separate file for "Letters Sent." You can organize your files by project and attach the letters you send with the responses.

It is also a good idea to have a separate file for contracts. Although you may not refer to this file very often, it will be easy to find when you need it. You can put the contracts in alphabetical order or some other order — you're in charge so make your own plan.

Whatever system you use, create one that works for you and change it when it no longer works. You will know how well it works by how hard it is to find things! If it takes you an hour to find a contract or a letter you wrote last month, your system needs to be rethought.

h. YOUR CLIPS

It is also a good idea to create a file of published clips because when you find a new client, invariably he or wants to see samples of your past work. If you have many clips, you can separate these into files of business articles, social science articles, etc. Or you can be more specific and separate them into articles on "Total quality management," "Egyptian hieroglyphics," and so on.

Incidentally, don't send your prospective clients originals of your clips if you can avoid it. Send photocopies and preserve the originals. Only send out originals if you have plenty of extra ones.

SAMPLE #15
TELEPHONE LOG

Date Called	Telephone Number	Charge	Client
5/23/9-	(555) 555-3333	$2.49	Joan Brown Marketing
5/23	(555) 555-9876	$7.87	Mark Heart Pres, ABC
5/24	(904) 555-3333	.48	Dr. Jones University of Florida

12
PROBLEM SITUATIONS AND COMMON MISTAKES

No matter how effective a writer and businessperson you are, problems will come up. This chapter concentrates on some common problems that writers face and possible ways to resolve them.

a. YOUR CLIENT HATES WHAT YOU WRITE

You thought the project was fine; your client does not. So what do you do?

I offer every client one free rewrite. But before I do, I need to know what the problem is. Does the editor want more quotes or more documentation? Is the article too short or too long? Maybe you've met the word count the client requested, but now he or she wants some adding or cutting.

Is the tone wrong? Were you humorous when you should have been serious? Did you write at too high or too low a reading level?

Get as many specifics as possible from your client so that you can fix the problem. There are those few clients who will never be satisfied, no matter what you or anyone else does. They are constantly rewriting and reorganizing and just can't let go of a project.

These editors don't usually last long because they drive their coworkers crazy. You will meet a few of them in the course of your career.

If you find that you are working with such an editor, satisfy him or her as much as possible. Once the job is done, you need never work with that person again, no matter how good the money is. The emotional strain is just not worth it.

b. SOMETIMES YOU WILL HAVE TO MISS A DEADLINE

I have called editors from the hospital to let them know a story will be late, and why.

Remember that editors are people and if you have a reasonable excuse for not finishing your work on time, they will usually understand.

As soon as you know that your work will probably be late, notify your client so he or she can make other arrangements. Perhaps you can have your research shipped to the client and another writer can take over the project. Or perhaps the editor can delay the project and allow you to finish it later on.

Be honest with the editor and in most cases, he or she will be fair and honest with you.

c. A CLIENT WANTS TO MONOPOLIZE YOUR TIME

This can be a nice kind of problem to have, even if it may not seem like it at the time. In some situations, clients like your work so much that they want to give you all the work they can. When you have too much work, you may have to give up other clients. Saying no is hard, especially when you have a client who likes you and pays well.

But it is important to remember that you must still spend at least 20% to 30% of your time marketing. You cannot depend on one client for all of your revenues. If something should happen to that client, and things can happen very fast in the business world, you'll be out of work.

d. COMMON MISTAKES

Probably the biggest mistake most new writers make is not realizing that writing is a business. I've spent most of this book discussing how and why you need to maintain a businesslike attitude to become a profit-making writer. Here are a few very common mistakes that both new and experienced writers tend to make.

1. Saying yes when you really mean no

When your revenues are directly dependent on the work you do, it is hard to turn down a job that pays well. But sometimes you just have to say no. You may not have the time to do this job because you have committed to other jobs. Don't sacrifice quality and your reputation by skimping on a job or short-changing a client.

The job may be interesting but not pay enough. Or perhaps you've been writing this column for two years and don't know how to tell the editor you just can't do it anymore. Carefully determine what are your most important and lucrative jobs and how much time various jobs take.

For example, in some cases a $200 magazine article is better than a $1,000 article for a national publication. How could this be? If the $200 article requires minimal research and takes you two hours to write, then you're earning $100 per hour. Perhaps the $1,000 article requires 60 hours or more. That means you'll earn $16.66 per hour. Sure, you'll gain prestige by having your work appear in a renowned publication. If the pay differential is worth it, then turn down the $200 job. However, be sure that you understand that more money doesn't always mean a better offer.

2. Agonizing over trivial details

This is a major time-waster among new writers. For example, if you sent a letter to an agent and also to a publisher about an idea you have and each responds and is interested, what should you do?

Unless you have a contract with the agent, you have a right to send the material to the publisher. You could send it directly to the agent and delay sending to the publisher. (Although I'd probably recommend the reverse. It is, after all, the publisher who is your ultimate customer.)

To avoid these dilemmas, plan ahead and set policies for yourself. Presume that everyone who receives your letter will be immediately thrilled and eager to learn more. This will help you judge whom to send queries to and how many letters to send.

3. Not trusting your instincts

Although I strongly believe it's important to think rationally and clearly, I also acknowledge that we all have an internal system that processes subconscious and preconscious information. These are your gut feelings; it is important to listen to them.

Sometimes a project sounds perfect. The pay is generous, you like the client, the client's reputation is impeccable, and the terms and conditions of the agreement seem more than fair to you. Yet a nagging doubt persists; something in you says, "maybe not."

I'm not talking about the fear that most of us suffer at some point when we take on new challenges and do things we've never done before. Fears of inadequacy can be overcome. Instead, I'm referring to those times when there is something wrong, but just can't pin it down. When that happens, I recommend you hold off. Delay accepting the job for at least a day or two until you can determine if it is really right for you.

4. Being dazzled by a high offer

When the editor or customer offers you a fee in the thousands, and you've been used to receiving hundreds, it is easy to feel "blown away" and that you must accept this job.

No matter how much money you are offered, it is always important to take into account how much work this project will take. How many hours over what period of time? Will the client expect you to dump your other customers and dedicate all your time to him or her?

Is there a potential for continued work with this client or is this a one-time deal? If you do accept the job and drop all your other clients for a period of time, do you think they'll still be there waiting for you later on?

How much up-front money is involved? If the answer is zero and yet this project is a long-term one for a considerable period, then what is in it for you?

This doesn't mean that big offers must always be looked at askance or that they inevitably mean trouble. But many writers are far more likely to jump on the bandwagon and accept without thinking because they are dazzled by the dollars. Don't make that mistake.

5. Ignoring or rationalizing ethical dilemmas

The more successful you become, the more likely you are to encounter at least a few ethical dilemmas.

You may be asked to write for a client who you don't like or who you may even consider disreputable. A client may ask you to do something that doesn't seem right to you.

A client in another country asked me to write about American electronic firms. It sounded like industrial espionage to me and I turned it down.

Some writers write term papers and doctoral dissertations for students. I have been offered such opportunities and have turned them down. They rationalize that politicians and actors hire ghostwriters all the time. However, in my view, it is popularly known that scripts are written for politicians and actors, but when it comes to receiving a Master's degree or a Ph.D., it is assumed that the student actually did the work.

There are also lesser ethical dilemmas; for example, is it okay to share information about one editor with another? It depends. Not if they are direct or even indirect competitors, in my opinion.

If they are not competitors, sometimes you can enhance your networking by telling other editors what projects you are working on. One of my editors sent me clippings on a subject I was researching for someone else, and they turned out to be very valuable to me.

It is also a good idea, incidentally, when you receive such good cooperation from an editor to reciprocate by sending clips that might be interesting and helpful to his or her own work.

There are many possible mistakes that writers can make; I've tried to summarize the key ones. So avoid making these mistakes, instead, forge ahead and make different and less costly ones! Mistakes are unavoidable and a necessary part of learning the business. Everyone makes a few mistakes now and then.

13
HAVE A LIFE!

When you're working on a particularly fascinating article or project, it is easy to lose track of time and forget the basics like sleeping, eating, and so on.

Don't chain yourself to your computer. You'll hurt your back and I suspect your mind may atrophy as well.

When you become very involved with a project, you can also become obsessed, which is okay in the short term. However, don't forget to enjoy your life.

A good writer is also a well-rounded person. Get some exercise, go for a walk, or go to the gym. Take your kids for a trip. Visit another city and gain a new perspective. Live!

Although there will be days when you really must work long hours in order to get a project done, this should not be a way of life, day-in, day-out. You could rapidly become burned out this way. In my opinion, this is one major drawback to working at home: becoming obsessed about working hard.

So if the only way to tear yourself away from work is to actually schedule time alone or with your spouse or kids, then do so. Remember that staff employees are given periodic breaks and time off for lunch and you should be at least as kind to yourself.

In this book I've forewarned you sufficiently so you can avoid many mistakes and problems. Freelance writing can be very rewarding, but keep in mind that it is a business.

I hope you find your writing business intriguing and profitable. Today is the information age. More than ever, people need clear, concise, accurate, well-written information. This need can only accelerate; as a writer, you can be an important and integral part of this very exciting era.

I'd like to know how you have done. Please write to me care of Self-Counsel Press at the address below:

Self-Counsel Press
1481 Charlotte Road
North Vancouver, British Columbia
Canada V7J 1H1
or

Self-Counsel Press
1704 N. State Street
Bellingham, Washington 98225

APPENDIX
PUBLICATIONS FOR WRITERS

a. BOOKS

The Complete Guide to Self-Publishing by Marilyn and Tom Ross
Writer's Digest Books
1507 Dana Avenue
Cincinnati, OH 45207
A very detailed and useful handbook on self-publishing.

Insider's Guide to Book Editors, Publishers, and Literary Agents
Jeff Herman
Prima Publishing
P.O. Box 1260BK
Rocklin, CA 95677
Tel: (916) 786-0426
This book is a must for those interested in book publishing. Lists book editors and agents and their interests.

The Self-Publishing Manual
Dan Poynter
Para Publishing
P.O. Box 4232
Santa Barbara, CA 93140-4232
Tel: (805) 968-7277
A lot of "hand-holding" and practical advice for self-publishers.

b. MAGAZINES AND NEWSLETTERS

1. United States

ByLine Magazine
P.O. Box 130596
Edmond, OK 73013

Freelance Success
42 Hicks Street 4N
Brooklyn Heights, NY 11201-6906
(718) 625-5577
Listings for key markets, special reports, and good articles.

Freelance Writer's Report
Cassell Communications
Maple Ridge Road
North Sandwich, NH 03259
Monthly newsletter with market listings
Tel:(800) 351-9278 (toll-free in U.S. and Canada)

Publishers Weekly
249 W. 17th Street
New York, NY 10011
Weekly, concentrates on book industry.

The Writer
120 Boston Street
Boston, MA 02116
Monthly, heavier concentration on fiction.

Writer's Digest
1507 Dana Avenue
Cincinnati, OH 45207
Tel: (513) 531-8250
Published monthly, heavy on helpful how-to information for beginners.

Writer's Journal
3585 N. Lexington Avenue, Suite 328
Arden Hills, MN 55126-8056

Writing for Money
Blue Dolphin Communications, Inc.
86 Old Sudbury Road
Wayland, MA 01778
Tel: (508) 358-7661
Published 17 times per year. I've obtained
very good leads from this publication.

2. Canada

Canadian Writer's Journal
Box 6618
Dept. 1
Victoria, B.C.
Canada V8P 5N7
Quarterly magazine.

c. ORGANIZATIONS FOR WRITERS

1. United States

American Medical Writers Association
9650 Rockville Pike
Bethesda, MD 20814-3998
Tel: (301) 493-0003

American Society of Journalists & Authors
Suite 302, 1501 Broadway
New York, NY 10036
Tel: (212) 997-0947

Association of Desktop Publishers
#800, 4677 30th Street
San Diego, CA 92116-3245

The Authors Guild
330 W. 42nd Street
New York, NY 10036

Editorial Freelancers Association
Room 9R, 36 E. 23rd Street
New York, NY 10159-2050

Freelance Editorial Association
P.O. Box 380835
Cambridge, MA 02238-9998

International Association of Business
Communicators
Suite 600, 1 Hallidie Plaza
San Francisco, CA 94102
Tel: (415) 433-3400

National Writers Association
Suite 424, 1450 S. Havana
Aurora, CO 80012
Tel: (303) 751-7844

PEN American Center
568 Broadway
New York, NY 10003
Tel: (212) 334-1660

Publication Services Guild
P.O. Box 19663
Atlanta, GA 30325

Public Relations Society of America
33 Irving Place
New York, NY 10003-2376
Tel: (212) 995-2230

Society for Technical Communication
901 N. Stuart Street, Suite 904
Arlington, VA 22203-1854
Tel: (703) 522-4114

Society of American Business Editors &
Writers, Inc.
c/o Janine Latus-Musick
University of Missouri
School of Journalism
P.O. Box 838
Columbia, MO 65205
Tel: (314) 882-7862

Society of Professional Journalists
16 S. Jackson
Greencastle, IN 46135

Women in Communications, Inc. (WICI)
3717 Columbia Pike, Suite 310
Arlington, VA 22204-4255
Tel: (703) 920-5555

Writers Connection
P.O. Box 24770
San Jose, CA 95154-4770
Tel: (408) 445-3600

2. Canada

Canadian Association of Journalists
Carleton University
St. Patrick's Building
1125 Colonel By Drive
Ottawa, Ontario
K1S 5B6

Canadian Authors Association
#500, 275 Slater Street
Ottawa, Ontario
K1P 5H9
Tel: (613) 233-2846

Editors' Association of Canada
35 Spadina Road
Toronto, Ontario
M5R 2S9
Tel: (416) 975-1379

Periodical Writers Association
of Canada (PWAC)
24 Ryerson Avenue, 1st Floor
Toronto, Ontario
M5T 2P3
Tel: (416) 868-6913

Writers' Union of Canada
24 Ryerson Avenue
Toronto, Ontario
M5T 2P3
Tel: (416) 868-6914

d. COMPUTER SERVICES

BRS Information Technologies
BRS Search Service
8000 Wespark Drive
McLean, VA 22102

CompuServe
5000 Arlington Center Boulevard
P.O. Box 20212
Columbus, OH 43220
Tel: (800) 848-8199 (toll-free in U.S. and Canada)

DIALOG Information Services, Inc.
33460 Hillview Avenue
Palo Alto, CA 94304
Tel: (415) 858-7069

GEnie
401 N. Washington Street
Rockville, MD 20850
Tel: (301) 340-4000

Information Access Company/Predicasts
11001 Cedar Avenue
Cleveland, OH 44016
Tel: (216) 795-3000

Prodigy Services Co.
445 Hamilton Avenue
White Plains, NY 10650
Tel: (914) 448-2496

UMI/Data Courier
620 S. Third Street
Louisville, KY 40202
Tel: (502) 583-4111

University Microfilms International
300 North Zeeb Road
Ann Arbor, MI 48105
Tel: (313) 761-4700

e. SELECTED PUBLISHERS, ORGANIZATIONS, AND DATABASES

1. United States

AT&T Toll Free 800 Directories
55 Corporate Drive
Room 24C36
Bridgewater, NJ 08807

Gale Research, Inc.
835 Penobscot Building
Detroit, MI 48226
Tel: (313) 961-2242

General Accounting Office
P.O. Box 6015
Gaithersburg, MD 20884-6015

Information USA, Inc.
3720 Farragut Avenue
P.O. Box E
Kensington, ME 20895
Tel: (301) 942-6303

National Technical Information Service
5285 Port Royal Road
Springfield, VA 22161
Tel: (703) 487-4600

The New York Times
229 West 43rd Street
New York, NY 10036
Tel: (212) 556-1573

Special Libraries Association
1700 18th Street NW
Washington, DC 20009
Tel: (202) 234-4700

Department of Labor/Bureau of Labor
Statistics
U.S. Department of Commerce
Economics and Statistics Administration
Washington, DC 20230
Tel: (202) 482-1986

United Nations Publications
United Nations
New York, NY 10017
Tel: (212) 963-7680

United States Government Printing Office
Superintendent of Documents
Washington, DC 20402
Tel: (202) 783-3238

2. Canada

Intercultural Systems
P.O. Box 588, Station B
Ottawa, Ontario
K1P 5P7
Tel: (613) 238-6169

Statistics Canada
Statistical Reference Center
R.H. Coats Building Lobby
Holland Avenue
Ottawa, Ontario
K1A 0T6
Tel: (613) 951-8116

W.I.S.E.R. Research
8955 13th Avenue, Suite 5
Montreal, Quebec
H1Z 3L1

f. SERVICES THAT USE TECHNICAL WRITERS

CDI Corporation
1717 Arch Street
Philadelphia, PA 19103-2768
Tel: (215) 569-2200
800-JOB-LINE
Experienced engineers preferred.

MiniSystems
124 West Figueroa Street
Santa Barbara, CA 93101
Tel: (805) 963-9660
PDS Technical Services
P.O. Box 619820
Dallas, TX 75261
Tel: (214) 621-8080
1 (800) 270-4737
Wants experienced writers for software
documentation

Techwrights, Inc.
540 Route 10 West, Suite 314
Randolph, NJ 07869
Tel: (201) 786-7244
Covers the Hartford, CT to Philadelphia
area

GLOSSARY

ADVANCE

An amount an author receives against royalties. Not all publishers pay advances. If an author receives, for example, a $5,000 advance, this amount is deducted from later earnings of the book and is reported on the royalty statement.

Therefore, if the book earns back $5,100 in royalties accrued over a six-month period (based on the royalty percentage the author and publisher have agreed upon), then the author will receive a check for $100.

CLIPS OR CLIPPINGS

Pieces that you have already written and had published. Although some writers send manuscript sheets to potential customers or markets, many photocopy previously published pieces and send them along with a query letter.

Don't send your article on illicit sex to a religious publication and don't send a clip about the power of prayer to a men's publication that you want to write for. Instead, gauge what you send to what you think your potential customer wants.

CONTRACT

Written or verbal agreement between writer and publisher or editor (or businessperson, individual, etc.) to do work. Whenever possible, *get it in writing*. There is too much room for confusion otherwise.

DEADLINE

This is when the article, book, or project is due. Although some editors give an earlier-than-needed deadline to the writer, many tell the writer exactly when the piece is needed.

If space is saved for a writer's piece and it doesn't arrive on time, it creates extra work for an editor and a time crunch. He or she won't hire you again unless you have a very good reason for being late.

Tell an editor up front if you're running into a problem or can't complete a job on time so that he or she can suggest a solution or make other plans.

EXPENSES

Writers should always ask magazine editors and other contacts if they will be reimbursed for expenses. (Book authors are usually not reimbursed, although some writers do make such arrangements.)

Many editors will reimburse expenses for phone, postage, express mail, fax, interview, and travel outside your local area. Telephone expenses are based on actual costs and travel expenses vary with the client. Some editors will reimburse for overnight expenses and some will even give you their Federal Express number.

FIRST DRAFT

Implies that you are willing to make changes that your customer requests.

GRAF OR 'GRAPH

Paragraph.

INVOICE

A bill to the editor or publisher, listing the fee for the work and any reimbursable expenses. Some writers are horrified at the thought of submitting an invoice.

Most editors and other customers consider invoices to be quite routine. In some cases, editors can give writers a purchase order number which must be placed on the invoice. This means they have budgeted ahead for your article, which is good!

Generally, invoices are paid within about 30 days. State 30 days as your term of payment unless you have an agreement to be paid immediately.

Note: Be sure to include your name and address on the invoice so the customer will know who to pay. Also, provide a few words or a sentence describing the project.

KILL FEE
The amount editor or publisher agrees ahead of time to pay the writer if the piece is not published. Usually it is a percentage of whatever amount would have been paid had the article been published, for example, 20% or 30%.

MANUSCRIPT OR MS.
Refers to your written material.

MARKET
Refers to where you plan to sell the piece. Your market may be travel magazines or health periodicals or retirement publications, depending on who you see as your ultimate readers. The word market is also used in book publishing to refer to those who you anticipate will buy the book you plan to write.

ON SPECULATION (ON SPEC)
This means you agree to write a piece that the editor may or may not publish, depending on whether he or she likes it or not. New writers often accept such terms to penetrate difficult markets.

PAYMENT ON ACCEPTANCE
This means you will receive your money when the editor formally accepts the piece, which may coincide with when the piece is published, but usually means you are paid sooner. Clarify with each editor what he or she means by this term.

PAYMENT ON PUBLICATION
One might think that the day your article is published, then that is the day your check is sent out. In the real world, it may well mean 30 or even 60 days later.

PAYMENT PER WORD
Many editors pay authors by word count. Thus, if they pay $1 per word and want 1,000 words, then they will pay $1,000. Note that this is usually per edited word, to avoid writers padding their copy to up the ante.

QUERY LETTER OR QUERY
A letter describing an article or book you would like to write. Some writers prefer the term "proposal." Queries for articles should be no more than one page, single-spaced.

RIGHTS
This subject basically refers to what you have agreed to sell to your customer. If your customer buys "all rights," then that means you can't sell the piece to anyone else. If he or she buys "first rights," then you may sell the piece as a "reprint" to another customer, usually a non-competing publication.

Many writers sell the same piece over and over to different markets, while others use the same research to reslant and rewrite the article.

ROYALTY
A term used in book publishing which refers to a percentage of the receipts earned on book sales the author will receive. Royalties may be based on the selling price of a book, or net sales, or many other variables. Royalty statements are usually provided to authors semi-annually or annually.

SASE
Self-addressed stamped envelope. Many magazine editors and publishers request that you enclose a SASE with your query or book proposal.

SLANT
Refers to the key thread underlying your article or written piece. For example, for an article about parenting, your basic subject may be how parents over 40 with new babies differ from parents in their twenties. Your slant may be on the psychological effects of kids on older parents versus younger parents. It could be on the health of older parents versus younger parents, or how children who are now grown up viewed their parents at these ages.

The slant of an article or piece is very important because it determines what research you use. It encompasses viewpoint as well. You may presume ahead of time that older parents are "better" or "worse" and your editor may ask you to find supporting evidence.

WORD COUNT

Most editors know approximately how long they want a written piece to be. It could be 500 words, 1,000 words, 2,000 words, or more.

Usually, the length is expressed in hundreds or thousands of words. A double-spaced page of copy contains about 250 words. Many computer programs can calculate a word count for you.

The editor may edit your work down from what was requested. It is important to note that newspaper editors often use the term "column inch," which refers to the number of words in an inch of column space.

If you want to know how many words that is, find a copy of the publication and measure it off in one-inch squares, then count the number of words in that block. Each publication varies, because of type fonts and styles, etc.

ADDITIONAL TITLES IN THE SELF-COUNSEL SERIES

HOW TO INTERVIEW
The art of the media interview
Paul McLaughlin

Professional interviewers — on radio, TV, and in print — make interviewing look so easy. How do they do it? Does being a good interviewer depend on having the "right" personality? Or is it simply a matter of learning a set of techniques that guarantee success every time?

Author Paul McLaughlin draws on the experience of the professionals to examine the art of effective listening, the importance of reseach, pointers on obtaining interviews, how to prepare questions, and the specialized requirements of print and broadcast interviews. A highlight of each chapter is the feature interview with well-known interviewers such as Patrick Watson, George Plimpton, and Barbara Frum. $9.95

Some of the topics explored in this book are:

- Where to track down research material
- How to line up interviews
- How to use other sources to develop a profile of the interviewee
- Why you shouldn't be afraid of silence
- How tone of voice can affect your interview
- The best locations to choose for your interview

PRODUCING A FIRST-CLASS NEWSLETTER
A guide to planning, writing, editing, designing, photography, production, and printing
Barbara A. Fanson

Today, anyone with a computer can produce a well-designed newsletter.

Fanson, an award-winning newsletter publisher, deals with every step, from page layout to production schedules, editing to typesetting. Also, there are valuable suggestions on writing, choosing photos and graphics, and working with a printer.

This is the definitive book on newsletter publishing, one that shows how to create a professional-quality product to keep information flowing and staff motivated. $14.95

Contents include:

- Planning: getting your newsletter started
- What kind of newsletter do you need?
- Planning with a purpose
- Format: setting a style
- Building a functional format
- What you need to know about type
- Color
- Content: informing and entertaining the reader
- Good writing for great newsletters
- Writing headlines
- Legal considerations
- Desktop publishing and some basic elements of design

LEARN TO TYPE FAST
Completely new, easy method for beginners
Barbara Aliaga

A fast new method for learning to type.

This book takes the mystique out of learning to type. The author, after years of teaching typing, has devised a unique method for learning to type that eliminates the frustration and tedium found in most how-to-type books.

By using this new system, you can learn to type in five hours! Short review sessions serve to reinforce the basic skills learned in ten half-hour lessons. The system is based on learning the typewriter or computer keys in relation to your fingers, rather than the keyboard. This means you can learn the keys quickly and automatically even if you aren't at the keyboard! $12.95

This book also includes the following:

- How to use the finger labelling method
- Ten wall charts to use for each lesson
- The four common characteristics of good typists
- How to measure your progress
- How to do tabulations and number typing
- How to do centering and set up letter styles
- What you need to know about a computer or word processor keyboard

PREPARING A SUCCESSFUL BUSINESS PLAN
A practical guide for small business
Rodger Touchie, B.Comm., M.B.A.

At some time, every business needs a formal business plan. Whether considering a new business venture or rethinking an existing one, an effective plan is essential to success. From start to finish, this working guide outlines how to prepare a plan that will win potential investors and help achieve business goals.

Using worksheets and a sample plan, readers learn how to create an effective plan, establish planning and maintenance methods, and update their strategy in response to actual business conditions. $14.95

Contents include:

- The basic elements of business planning
- The company and its product
- The marketing plan
- The financial plan
- The team
- Concluding remarks and appendixes
- The executive summary
- Presenting an impressive document
- Common misconceptions in business planning
- Your business plan as a tangible asset

A SMALL BUSINESS GUIDE TO DIRECT MAIL
Build your customer base and boost profits
Lin Grensing

Do you want to get the most out of your marketing dollars? Direct mail could be the answer for you. Direct mail allows you to target specific customers and see immediately if your message is getting across. No other form of advertising allows you to measure your response so accurately and easily.

Direct mail produces results, and it's neither a difficult marketing technique nor beyond the means of the average small business owner. $9.95

The book answers questions like —

- How can I organize my own direct-mail campaign?
- How do I determine who my best potential customers are?
- How do I compile a mailing list?
- What postal requirements must I follow?
- What's the best way to chart my response rate and keep my mailing list up-to-date?
- What are the components of a successful direct-mail letter?
- What's the best way to design the order form?
- How can I develop good customer relations and stay in touch with my best customers?

MARKETING YOUR PRODUCT
A planning guide for small business
Donald Cyr, M.B.A. and
Douglas Gray, B.A., LL.B.

Learn the secrets of successful product marketing. Marketing is not just selling and advertising; its objectives are to help you decide if you are developing the right product for the right target market and if you are using the promotion vehicles and distribution methods to maximize the return on your efforts.

The in-depth checklists included in this book will take you, step by step, toward a successful, profitable marketing strategy. $12.95

It helps you determine the answers to questions such as:

- What is marketing?
- How do you plan a marketing strategy?
- How do you find out who your market is?
- Can you do your own market research?
- How do you develop your product to fit the market?
- Which media do you use to let your market know about your product?
- What makes people choose one product over another?
- Are promotions useful marketing tools?
- What is the best way to get your product to your customer?
- How do you price to sell?
- What advertising strategies are most effective for your product?
- What legal and insurance considerations must you be aware of?

PRACTICAL TIME MANAGEMENT
How to get more things done in less time
by Bradley C. McRae

Here is sound advice for anyone who needs to develop practical time management skills. It is designed to help any busy person, from any walk of life, use his or her time more effectively. Not only does it explain how to easily get more things done, it shows you how your self-esteem will improve in doing so. More important, emphasis is placed on maintenance so that you remain in control. Whether you want to find extra time to spend with your family or read the latest bestseller, this book will give you the guidance you need — without taking up a lot of your time! $7.95

Some of the skills you will learn are:

- Learning to monitor where your time goes
- Setting realistic and attainable goals
- Overcoming inertia
- Rewarding yourself
- Planning time with others
- Managing leisure time
- Finding time for physical fitness
- Planning time for hobbies and vacations
- Maintaining the new you

All prices are subject to change without notice. Books are available in book, department, and stationery stores. If you cannot buy the book through a store, please use this order form. (Please print)